1862-3.

AMERICAN EXPRESS COMPANY,

WESTERN DIVISION,

RULES, REGULATIONS & INSTRUCTIONS,

WITH THE

General Western Tariff,

INCLUDING, ALSO, THE TARIFF TO PRINCIPAL POINTS

OF CONNECTING EXPRESS COMPANIES.

NOTICE.—Employees to whom this Tariff is furnished are requested to preserve and pass it over to their successors, upon leaving the employ.

The Instructions and Tariff, with other matter contained herein, is in no case intended for the information of the public, nor as an advertisement; the Company reserving the right to vary from them at pleasure.

CHICAGO:
BEACH & BARNARD, PRINTERS, NO. 14 SOUTH CLARK STREET.

1862.

INDEX.

ORGANIZATION.

AMERICAN EXPRESS COMPANY.

ESTABLISHED 1840—ORGANIZED 1850—RE-ORGANIZED 1860.

Directors.

HENRY WELLS, Aurora, New York.
JOHN BUTTERFIELD, Utica, New York.
JOHNSTON LIVINGSTON, New York.
WM. G. FARGO, Buffalo, New York.
ALEX. HOLLAND, New York.
JOHN M. THOMPSON, Springfield, Mass.
JAS. C. FARGO, Chicago, Ill.

Officers.

HENRY WELLS, President.
JOHN BUTTERFIELD, Vice President.
WILLIAM G. FARGO, Secretary.
ALEXANDER HOLLAND, Treasurer.

Managing Directors.

ALEX. HOLLAND, Manager Eastern Division, New York.
JOHN M. THOMPSON, Manager New England Division, Springfield, Mass.
WM. G. FARGO, Manager Western Division, Buffalo, New York.
JAS. C. FARGO, Assistant Manager Western Division, Chicago, Ills.

Superintendents.

CHAS. H. WELLS, Superintendent Eastern Division, New York.
R. L. JOHNSON, Superintendent New England Division, Albany, N. Y.
J. H. ARNETT, Superintendent Canada Division, Hamilton, C. W.
J. G. BARNES, Superintendent Ohio Division, Cleveland, Ohio.
E. W. SLOAN, Superintendent Indiana Division, Indianapolis, Ind.
CHAS. FARGO, Superintendent Michigan Division, Detroit, Mich.
E. HAYDEN, Superintendent Illinois Division, Chicago, Ill.
B. P. PECKHAM, Superintendent Wisconsin Division, Milwaukee, Wis.
THOS. ADAMS, Superintendent Iowa Division, Dubuque, Iowa.

WM. HEWITT, Superintendent Union Line Express, Cleveland, Ohio.

American Express Company,

WESTERN DIVISION.

OFFICE OF THE MANAGING DIRECTOR,
Buffalo, Oct. 1, 1862.

To Superintendents, Agents, Messengers, and other employees of the Company, Western Division:

GENTLEMEN :—The Rules, Instructions, and Tariffs, with other information given herein, for the guidance of the Company's employees in this Division, are made up in part from those adopted at different times heretofore, with such changes and additions as appear necessary in the transaction of the business at this time. They are now issued in connection with the ***General Western Tariff,*** in order to have the same always at hand for reference and information.

As the nature of our business is one of *detail,* we have been obliged to make the Rules and Instructions explicit; and it is expected that each and every employee of the Company *will make the same his study;* and no plea of *ignorance* will be received as an excuse for mistakes in transacting any part of the business.

WM. G. FARGO,
Managing Director Western Division.

JAS. C. FARGO,
Assistant Managing Director, Chicago, Ill.

American Express Company.

BUSINESS OF THE COMPANY—THE TERRITORY OCCUPIED—DIVISION OF SAME, AND PLAN OF MANAGEMENT.

The business of the Company consists in the forwarding by passsenger trains, and other rapid modes of conveyance, merchandize, freight, parcels, valuable packages, jewelry, bank-notes, gold, silver, valuable papers, bonds, &c., and delivering the same at the place of business, or residence of the consignee, making collections with or without goods, the filling of orders, and attending to commissions generally.

The territory over which the Company run their Express extends from New York and Boston in the East, to the principal cities and towns in the States of Massachusetts, Vermont, New Hampshire, New York, Pennsylvania, Ohio, Northern Kentucky, Indiana, Michigan, Illinois, Wisconsin, Missouri, Iowa, and Canada West, occupying for its business the following railroad, lake, river and stage routes:

Eastern Division.

Hudson River Railroad.
New York Central Railroad and Branches:
Including Main Line—Albany to Buffalo.
" Branches—Schenectady to Troy.
Syracuse to Rochester.
Rochester to Niagara Falls and Suspension Bridge.
Rochester to Charlotte.
Canandaigua to Batavia and Tonawanda.

Eastern Division.

New York Central—Batavia to Attica.
Buffalo to Lockport and Niagara Falls.
Black River and Utica Railroad.
Rome, Watertown and Ogdensburg Railroad.
Oswego and Syracuse Railroad.
Cooperstown and Cherry Valley (Stage Co.).
Cayuga Lake.
Seneca Lake.
Rochester and Port Hope (Lake Ontario).

New England Division.

Boston and Worcester Railroad.
Connecticut River Railroad.
Pittsfield and North Adams Railroad.
Western Railroad.
Vermont and Massachusetts Railroad.
(South Vernon to Brattleboro.)
Vermont Valley Railroad.
(Brattleboro to Bellows Falls.)
Ashuelot Railroad.
North Adams and Williamston (Stage).

Western Division.

CANADA SUB-DIVISION.

Buffalo and Lake Huron Railroad.
Grand Trunk Railroad (Sarnia to Toronto, and London Branch).
Great Western Railroad and Branches.
Including Main Line—Suspension Bridge to Detroit.
" Branches—Hamilton to Toronto.
Guelph to Harrisburgh.
London to Port Sarnia.
London to Port Stanley.

MICH. SUB-DIV.

Amboy, Lansing and Traverse Bay Railroad.
Michigan Central Railroad, (including Joliet Cut-off.)
Grand Trunk Railroad, (Detroit to Port Sarnia).

WESTERN DIVISION.

MICH. SUB-DIV.

Detroit and Milwaukee Railroad.
Grand Haven and Milwaukee (Steamship Line).
Detroit and Cleveland (Lake Erie).
Detroit and Port Huron (St. Clair River).

OHIO SUB-DIVISION.

Central Ohio Railroad (Zanesville to Columbus).
Cleveland, Columbus and Cincinnati Railroad.
Cleveland and Erie Railroad.
Buffalo and Erie Railroad.
Little Miami, Columbus and Xenia Railroad.
(Including Xenia and Springfield Branch)
Sunbury and Erie Railroad.
Erie and Pittsburg Railroad.
Philadelphia and Erie Railroad.
Coneautville and Meadville (Stage).
Cincinnati to Louisville (Ohio River).

INDIANA SUB-DIVISION.

Belfontaine Railroad.
Cincinnati, Hamilton and Dayton Railroad.
(Cincinnati to Hamilton.)
Cincinnati and Chicago Air Line Railroad.
Dayton, Xenia aud Belpre Railroad.
Eaton, Hamilton and Richmond Railroad.
Cincinnati and Indianapolis Junction Railroad.
Indiana Central and Dayton and Western Railroad.
Lafayette and Indianapolis Railroad.
Louisville, New Albany and Chicago Railroad.
Peru and Indianapolis Railroad.
Terre Haute and Richmond Railroad.
St. Louis, Alton and Terre Haute Railroad.

ILLINOIS SUB-DIV.

Chicago, Burlington and Quincy Railroad.
Illinois Central Railroad (Main Line).
Illinois Central Railroad (Chicago Branch).
Hannibal and St. Joseph Railroad.
Quincy and Chicago Railroad.

WESTERN DIVISION.

ILLINOIS SUB-DIV.

Pittsburg, Fort Wayne and Chicago Railroad.
Wabash and Mississippi Railroad.
Burlington and Missouri River Railroad.
Keokuk, Montrose and Mt. Pleasant Railroad.
St Louis to Keokuk (Mississippi River).
Fort Madison to Burlington (Mississippi River).

WISCONSIN SUB-DIVISION.

Chicago and Milwaukee Railroad.
Chicago and North Western Railroad.
La Crosse and Milwaukee Railroad.
Milwaukee and Western Railroad.
Milwaukee and Horricon Railroad.
Milwaukee and Prairie du Chien Railroad.
Racine and Mississippi Railroad.
Southern Wisconsin Railroad.
Kenosha, Rockford and Rock Island Railroad.
Northern Illinois Railroad.
Milwaukee to Sheboygan (Lake Mich. & Stage).

IOWA SUB-DIVISION.

Beloit and Madison Railroad.
Chicago, Fulton and Iowa Central Railroad.
Chicago, Iowa and Nebraska Railroad.
Cedar Rapids and Missouri Railroad.
Dubuque and Sioux City Railroad.
Dubuque and Western Railroad.
Fox River Valley Railroad.
Galena and Chicago Union Railroad.
Mineral Point Railroad.
Winfield and Naperville (Stage).
Dubuque to La Crosse (Mississippi River).

For the better convenience in managing the business, these lines (as marked) have been arranged into three divisions, viz., the "Eastern," "New England," and "Western."

The "Eastern Division" extends from New York to Buffalo and Suspension Bridge, and, during season of navigation, to Coburg, Colburne, Port Hope, and Kingston, C. W.

The "New England Division" extends from Boston to Albany and intermediate points, in the States of New York, Massachusetts, Vermont and New Hampshire.

The "Western Division" extends from Buffalo and Suspension Bridge westward, including Canada West, Western Pennsylvania, Michigan, Ohio, Indiana, Illinois, Northern Kentucky, Missouri, Iowa and Wisconsin.

In order to secure a prompt and efficient transaction of the business in so large a territory, the Western Division has been sub-divided into seven sections, or sub-divisions, as follows: "Canada," "Michigan," "Ohio," "Indiana," "Illinois," "Wisconsin," and "Iowa;" the management of each division being entrusted to a Division Superintendent, with headquarters at Hamilton, C. W., Detroit, Cleveland, Indianapolis, Chicago, Milwaukee and Dubuque; the Superintendents of the Canada, Ohio and Indiana Divisions acting under instructions from the Managing Director of Western Division at Buffalo, and the Michigan, Illinois, Wisconsin and Iowa Divisions under instructions from the Assistant Manager at Chicago.

In addition to the routes included in these three Divisions (Eastern, New England and Western), the Company own and control one-half of the "Union Line Express," extending from Cleveland and Crestline south and east to Pittsburg, and occupying for its business the following railroads and other routes:

Pittsburg, Fort Wayne and Chicago Railroad (Crestline to Pittsburg).

Cleveland and Pittsburg Railroad.

Cleveland, Zanesville and Cincinnati Railroad.

Cleveland and Mahoning Railroad (including Tuscarawas Branch).

Newcastle and Pittsburg Route.

This line is owned jointly by the American and Adams Express Companies, and is managed separate and independent of the business of either Company, under the charge of a Superintendent having his headquarters at Cleveland.

GENERAL REMARKS IN REFERENCE TO THE BUSINESS.

THE EXPRESS BUSINESS is eminently one of detail, requiring of all persons engaged in it, system, accuracy, punctuality, watchfulness, urbanity, *and, above all, that the business of to-day be done before to-morrow.* Among the prolific sources of loss to the Company are:

By goods being improperly *marked.*

By being improperly *packed* for safe carriage.

By carelessness in *handling.*

By receiving goods of little or no value, and forwarding without pre-payment, and by advancing charges on them.

By carelessness in giving receipts.

By neglecting to notify back when goods are *short.*

By neglecting to carefully check.

By want of uniformity in charges, causing dissatisfaction to the customer.

By want of courtesy, and attention to the interests of customers; consequently injuring the popularity of the Company.

By carelessness in the safe keeping of money and other valuable packages.

By neglecting to adjust promptly all claims for loss or damage.

By neglecting to properly waybill money packages.
By loss or misplacement of safe and trunk keys.
By suffering C. O. D. goods to be delivered before payment of bill.
By neglecting to take receipts for goods delivered.
By neglecting to return collections when made.
By neglecting to keep watch of money and valuable packages, when in wagons.

To obviate these evils, and to insure, so far as practicable, uniformity in all departments throughout the entire business of the Company, strict observance of the following rules is enjoined upon all the employees of the Company, affording due allowance for the exercise of a sound discretion.

GENERAL INSTRUCTIONS TO DIVISION SUPERINTENDENTS.

1. The Division Superintendents represent the Company in their respective positions, and are subject only to the instructions of the General Superintendent of the Division.

2. The appointment and discharge of agents, clerks, messengers, drivers, or other employees, will be made by the Division Superintendents in their respective Divisions.

3. No employee discharged from one Division must be employed in another, without the approval of the Superintendent who discharged him.

4. You will, as often as practicable, visit each office in your Division, for the purpose of affording instruc-

tions, giving counsel and information, looking into accounts, and investigating the manner in which the business is conducted.

5. You are expected to see that no larger force is kept at an office, or on any route, than is necessary for the prompt and economical transaction of the business, and that no person is continued in the employ whose private acts or character tend to injure the good name of the Company.

6. In authorizing purchases of fixtures, or personal property, you will make yourselves acquainted with the necessity of the same before granting the authority, and all vouchers for such expenses must be approved by you in writing.

7. All contracts with transportation lines, with bankers, or others, for season contracts, all offices opened or discontinued, agents, messengers or men employed or discharged, and in fact a general report of your transactions must be made to the General Superintendent of your Division weekly.

8. In opening new, or closing old offices, notice must be given to *all offices and messengers* under *your supervision,* stating name of place, and tariff to same; or if for closing an office, state to *what point* such matter must be *billed thereafter.*

9. At points where the Company have horses and wagons, Superintendents will make it their particular business to see that such property is kept in good condition, and as well and economically taken care of as possible.

10. They will be particular to see that freight is handled carefully by the respective agents, messengers and drivers in their Division, and where damage occurs from

carelessness, either collect the amount of damage from the employee causing said damage, or discharge him.

GENERAL INSTRUCTIONS TO AGENTS.

1. Agents will observe the instructions of the Division Superintendent of their Division, in all matters appertaining to the business of the Company. Letters, or matters connected with the *business of a Division*, should be addressed to the *Division Superintendent*; those of a *general nature* to the *General Superintendent*. All communications should be *promptly answered in writing*.

2. Clerks, Drivers and Messengers will be subject to the direction and instruction of the Agent at the office where employed.

3. When good cause is given, Agents will suspend from duty Messengers running from, or any person employed in, their office, and consult the Division Superintendent as to further action.

4. Never *mention* to any one the amount of money received or forwarded. *Secrecy is half the safety* in the Express business. Keep the safes at all times where they will be inaccessible to persons not employed by the Company. *Never allow any one behind the counters*, except those of our own men *having business* there; and when sending off, or receiving a money run, allow *no one* within reach but the Messenger. The business of the Company, and the transactions of its customers through your office, *must be confidential*. Books, bills, &c., *are not* to be open for public inspection. Preserve carefully all letters,

books and papers connected with the business. Particular care must be taken that the property of the Company is not abused or damaged by neglect of proper repairs. This applies particularly to horses, wagons, harness and sleighs.

5. *Be careful* in making *special agreements*, and always consult authority. *Always fulfill contracts* made by other Agents, whenever a *receipt*, with an agreement on it, or other *good evidence* is shown. When contracts are not in accordance with the tariff, *the receipt* should be taken from the holder and sent to the General Superintendent of the Division.

6. Agents will in *all cases* require freight and charges to be paid on delivery of goods, *except in cases of season contract*—("S. C.") When the consignee of a valuable package is unknown, *he must be identified* by some responsible person; and the person identifying *must sign with party receiving* upon the receipt book; and all receipts must be taken *under the date* on which the package is delivered. When packages are delivered upon written order of party to whom they are addressed, the order must be preserved by pasting same in back of receipt book upon which the article is receipted. Agents will be held personally responsible for the freight and charges on goods delivered at their respective offices, and should never send Drivers to *collect or deliver* large amounts of money, without experienced and competent assistance.

7. Agents failing to notify at once, offices from which goods are "short," will be held as having received them. On arrival of Messenger and goods, way-bills should be carefully checked, and if anything is short, mark opposite, "not received." Take immediate and effective steps to find the same. Write the office from which the missing article started, also any interme-

diate checking office, and notify Messenger. When money packages are short, or missing, telegraph and write immediately, same as above. Agents, at re-shipping points must keep such records of goods and way-bills passing through their offices as will enable them to be traced, if way-bills and goods get separated, as they do on long lines. Such offices must be prepared, in the way above indicated, to give the *time* the delayed goods passed through their hands.

8. Agents will require Messengers to receipt on Way-bill Register for all way-bills delivered them. At stations where trains do not stop a sufficient time for comparing way-bills with Register, before signing, agents will count the same, and enter the number received directly under their signature. Where there is time before trains leave, the way-bills and Way-bill Register must be compared to see that they agree, and also the way-bill with the package, giving notice to the Messenger on the spot, if any article on same is short, and requiring his signature to the fact on the way-bill.

9. When goods are received marked with a private mark, in all cases enter name of consignee in full upon the way-bill, with destination.

10. Goods evidently not worth the transportation, or that would not, under ordinary circumstances, sell for the charges, should not be received unless the charges are *pre-paid*, or guaranteed. Especial care should be taken, in advancing charges on goods, to know that they are worth charges and freight.

11. All packages containing poultry, fish, fruit, or perishable articles of any description, should have the character thereof distinctly marked upon them, as also the full address of the consignee, including street and number. When perishable goods are refused by consignee,

or not called for, (unless other instructions accompany them) they should be at once disposed of to the best advantage, after having consulted some judicious person, in the trade, as to the manner and propriety of so doing. Return an account of sales, with net proceeds, to the shipper, addressed to the office from which the goods came. If the shipper is not known, send account of sales to the Agent where shipped from, and ascertain who is entitled to the proceeds.

12. All goods not called for within *twenty-four hours* after being received, should be entered upon the "package on hand" book furnished for that purpose, and consignee notified through the post-office with the usual blanks. Every exertion should be made to deliver packages, and not allow them to accumulate.

13. Packages containing liquid in glass must only be received at owner's risk, and so specified in the receipt; and in order to have such contract for reference, in case of loss or damage, Agents will give a receipt and require a *duplicate*, with agreement and signature of shipper across face of same, assuming and agreeing to conditions given thereon.

14. When freight is prepaid, the person receiving the money will mark the package "paid," with his name or initials.

15. When claims for delays, breakage, damages, lost or stolen goods, are presented, the Agent should personally examine into the claim, and not refer it to Drivers or Clerks, a statement of the case should be sent to the Division Superintendent, asking for instructions. If suits are brought against the Company, immediately notify the Division Superintendent. A ready method to determine if any part of the contents of a package have been ab-

stracted, is to weigh and compare it with the original weight marked on the package.

16. Goods or articles addressed to the "care of" an individual, or Company, *must be delivered to that individual, or Company*, and not to the person to whom addressed. In delivering money packages and specie with the aid of our wagons, always carry them locked in a safe or trunk, and *constantly in sight.*

17. *Never contract* or receipt to *deliver* articles in a specified time, nor to *deliver* goods beyond the termination of our Express routes. (We only agree to hand them over to other Companies or forwarders in good standing, and take their receipt). In no instance will this Company take any responsibility, or be liable for loss or damage after the package is forwarded as directed, or handed over to other well known forwarders to complete the transportation and delivery.

18. *Never make a price* for forwarding an article, without seeing and knowing something of its weight, bulk, contents and value.

19. Packages for the *United States Mint and Patent Office must be prepaid,* and have the name of the consignor marked on them. Money to pay Patent Office charges, must be in *separate packages*, with name and address of consignor on them.

20. When forwarding valuable packages, note the value on the way-bill, and call the Messenger's attention to the fact, particularly when sent outside of trunk or safe.

21. Give a receipt for every *money package* received, and keep the packages *locked* in the *safe* until checked to Messenger. When sending off boxes or bags of coin too heavy to put in the safe, have the same entered on

the *freight*, in addition to the *money* bill. Take care that Messengers do not start without their way-bills.

22. The exact amount of money contained in packages, should be plainly marked on them. Parties sending *must* always count their money, and, if able, seal and address their own packages. No money package *must be receipted for* until after it is sealed.

23. Gold and silver *must not be taken in bags* in amounts over $2000 in gold, or $200 in silver; but *must be packed in boxes strapped with iron, top and bottom screwed*, and plainly *sealed with shippers' seal*, and weight of same marked upon the outside of package, together with the amount enclosed. Under these amounts coin may be received in bags, but the bag *must be examined closely*, to see whether there have been any repairs made to it, *whether it is securely tied, sealed, and in good condition generally;* if not, *refuse it.* All coin in bags or boxes, or packages of money of every kind, should be examined closely in passing from offices to Messengers, or Messengers to offices, and if there are any defects, call each other's attention to them, and note them on the way-bill, sign your name and office, and require Messengers to do the same.

24. Every money package put up in an envelope must have five seals upon it as follows: one on the centre, and one on each seam of the envelope, half way from the centre to the corner (see diagram.)

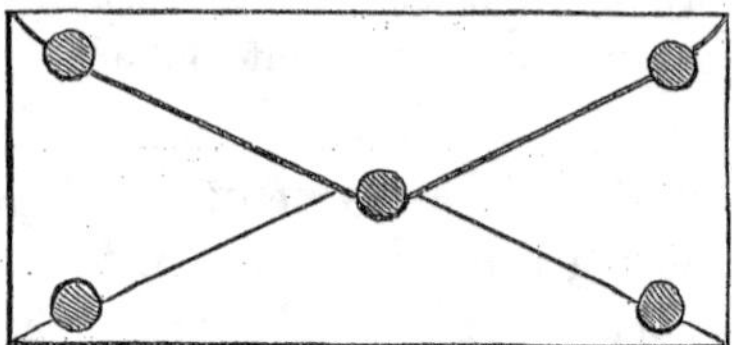

25. No package of money in an envelope must be allowed to leave an office without being thus sealed. Large packages of money, otherwise put up, must be so securely sealed that they can by no possibility be tampered with. If any error or short count occurs in packages not sealed in accordance with these instructions, the amount will be charged back to the Agent or office forwarding the same. (Messengers, for their own safety, will be allowed to refuse money packages not thoroughly and securely sealed.) All packages of coin should be carefully weighed, the weight marked on the package, and entered upon the way-bill. Should any office start coin and neglect this rule, the next office checking same *must weigh* and enter it on the way-bill, and no Agent or Clerk will be excused for allowing packages of coin to pass through the office without the weight being entered. All intermediate offices checking way-bills on which there is coin or gold-dust in transit, as well as the office delivering same, should verify the weight of each package on its arrival. By this means the robbery of a box or bag of coin may be immediately detected.

26. Anything different from the ordinary business of the Express Company should be declined, when there is risk of damage, or loss, from neglect of *extra* duty, &c., in performing the service correctly. Agents should prevent the Company from being made use of for fraudulent purposes.

27. *All employees* handling freight, are required to do their duty with such thoughtful care that the most frail article may be forwarded, by the *American Express Company*, with the certainty of being delivered entire and uninjured. To effect this, it is necessary that no article, of whatever description, be thrown, dropped, or allowed to fall, no matter how short the distance.

28. *Any employee* who may become cognizant of default in duty by another employee, and fails to report same to the Superintendent of his Division, becomes equally censurable with the defaulter.

29. A general tariff is furnished to each office, and must not be varied from except by consent of the General Superintendent. When new offices are opened, or old ones closed, Agents will be promptly notified of same, and must make the proper entry upon their tariff, filing the notice for future reference. *A special tariff* on game, furs, produce, &c., &c., will be issued by circular, from time to time, and must be pasted in back of general tariff for reference.

30. Special Messengers should not be sent off the main routes, excepting for very good reasons, which should be assigned to the Superintendent of the Division.

31. All blanks, stationery, and other articles necessary for the transaction of the business, will be furnished upon application to the principal office in the Division. Do not change the form of any of the blanks by tearing or pasting them together, nor allow them to be destroyed. In ordering stationery, you will name the number of blanks required, as per following list. Always write your orders for such supplies on the blank furnished for that purpose, and enclose in envelope addressed "order for stationery." For the purpose of saving time and trouble, you will, on or about the 20th of each month, make up your order for a sufficient supply to last during the month following. Orders for articles which have to be printed exclusively for your office, such as labels of all kinds, letter heads, blank receipts, collection envelopes, and way-bills, should be given at least one month before you wish to use them.

NOTE. Agents will return Messengers' Abstracts same as their own, except entering name of *Messenger* instead of office.

LIST OF BOOKS, BLANKS, &c., WITH NUMBERS OF SAME.

No. 1. Record of Way-bills received, 6 quires, full size.
No. 2. Record of Way-bills received, 2 quires, full size.
No. 3. Record of Way-bills received, 2 quires, half size.
No. 4. Record of Way-bills forwarded, 6 quires, full size.
No. 5. Record of Way-bills forwarded, 2 quires, full size.
No. 6. Record of Way-bills forwarded, 2 quires, half size.
No. 7. Record of Abstracts returned, 2 quires, for copying by press.
No. 8. Record of Abstracts returned, 2 quires, for copying by hand.
No. 9. Record of Abstracts returned, 3 quires, for copying by hand.
No. 10. Record of Abstracts returned, 4 quires, for copying by hand.
No. 11. Record of Statements returned, for copying by press.
No. 12. Record of Statements returned, 2 quires, for copying by hand.
No. 13. Record of Statements returned, 3 quires, for copying by hand.
No. 14. Record of Statements returned, 4 quires, for copying by hand.
No. 15. Record of Statements returned, 6 quires, for copying by hand.
No. 16. Record of Goods on hand, 2 quires, full size.
No. 17. Record of Goods on hand, 2 quires, half size.
No. 18. Delivery Receipt Book, canvass covered.
No. 19. Delivery Receipt Book, calf covered.
No. 20. Delivery Receipt Book, "Messenger's use."
No. 21. Delivery Receipt Book, "N. R. Agents' use."

No. 22. Blank Receipt Books, 100 bound receipts.
No. 23. Blank Receipt Books, 200 bound receipts.
No. 24. Blank Receipt Books, 300 bound receipts.
No. 25. Record of Way-bills passing offices, 2 quires, full size.
No. 26. Record of Way-bills passing offices, 3 quires, full size.
No. 27. Record of Way-bills passing offices, 2 quires, half size.
No. 28. Record of Way-bills carried by Messengers.
No. 29. Post Office Notice Books, 100 notices.
No. 30. Post Office Notice Books, 200 notices.
No. 31. Post Office Notice Books, 300 notices.
No. 32. Record of Collections forwarded.
No. 33. Record of Collections received.
No. 34. Record of Collections received and forwarded.
No. 35. Record of Freights transported, 100 pages.
No. 36. Record of Freights transported, 200 pages.
No. 37. Record of Freights transported, 300 pages.
No. 38. Record of Freights transported, 400 pages.
No. 39. Record of Season Contract Accounts.

BLANKS.

No. 40. Way-bills for Freight, full sheet.
No. 41. Way-bills for Freight, half sheet.
No. 42. Way-bills for Freight, quarter sheet.
No. 43. Way-bills for Money, full sheet.
No. 44. Way-bills for Money, half sheet.
No. 45. Way-bills for Money, quarter sheet.
No. 46. Way-bills for Messengers' "Duplicates."

No. 47. Blank Abstract of Way-bills, forwarded from office.

No. 48. Blank Abstract of Way-bills forwarded by Messengers.

No. 49. Blank Abstracts of Way-bills forwarded by temporary Messengers.

No. 50. Statements of Way-bills and Proceeds, returned to Buffalo office.

No. 51. Receipts for freight and money.

No. 52. Receipts for collections without goods.

No. 53. Monthly Freight Reports by office, half sheet.

No. 54. Monthly Freight Reports by office, full sheet.

No. 55. Daily Freight Reports by Messengers, full sheet.

No. 56. Daily Freight Reports by Messengers, half sheet.

No. 57. Vouchers for Messengers' Salary.

No. 58. Vouchers for Agents' Salary.

No. 59. Vouchers for N. R. Agents' Salary.

No. 60. Vouchers for Disbursements.

No. 61. Bill Heads for receipting charges to consignee.

No. 62. Enquiry Sheets for "short goods."

No. 63. Enquiry Sheets, C. O. D. goods refused.

No. 64. Letter Heads, full size.

No. 65. Letter Heads, commercial note.

No. 66. Monthly Balance Sheets.

No. 67. Monthly Report of goods on hand.

No. 68. Scrip Sheets.

No. 69. Daily Balance Reports.

No. 70. Order Blank for Stationery.

ENVELOPES.

No. 71. Money.
No. 72. Abstract.
No. 73. Statement.
No. 74. Collection, for C. O. D. goods.
No. 75. Collections, for collections without goods.
No. 76. Small printed.
No. 77. Large plain.
No. 78. Small plain.

MISCELLANEOUS ARTICLES.

No. 79. Labels, large, for freight.
No. 80. Labels, large, for C. O. D. freight.
No. 81. Labels, small, for C. O. D. packages.
No. 82. Labels, small, for ordinary packages.
No. 83. Labels, small, for money packages.
No. 84. Labels, route, for Messengers' use.
No. 85. Linen Tags, with eyelet holes.
No. 86. Wrapping paper, large, heavy.
No. 87. Wrapping paper, small, post office.
No. 88. Twine, heavy.
No. 89. Twine, light.
No. 90. Ink.
No. 91. Sealing Wax.
No. 92. Gum Arabic.
No. 93. National Tax Stamps.

RAILWAY EXPRESS AGENCY

INCORPORATED

RATE TABLE 1. BLOCK 742.

MAIN BLOCK TARIFF.

100	
Block	Scale
103	200
104	200
106	187
107	179
108	172
109	166
110	158
111	151
112	147
113	141
114	137
115	133
116	128
117	124
118	122
119	116
120	112
120½	112
121	107
121¼	109
121¾	107
122	101
122¼	105
122¾	101
123	99
123½	97
124	97
124½	93
125	93
126	88
127	86
128	86
129	82
130	84
131	88
132	82
133	74

200	
Block	Scale
201	208
203	196
204	191
205	187
206	179
207	175
208	170
209	170
209½	166
210	158
210½	158
211	158
213	141
214	137
215	137
215½	133
216	133
217	137
221	112
222	112
223	99
223½	97
224	93
224½	95
225	88
225¼	88
225¾	91
226	84
227	82
228	82
229	80
230	82
231	79
232	74
233	71
234	71
237	59
257	84
258	84

300	
Block	Scale
302	204
302½	208
303	200
305	183
306	179
307	179
308	175
309	175
311	154
312	149
313	141
314	137
315	128
316	120
317	120
318	116
318½	116
319	112
320	107
321	107
321½	103
322	101
322½	99
323	97
323½	95
324	93
324¼	95
324½	91
325	88
326	84
327	82
328	78
329	75
330	74
331	72
332	71
333	68
334	65
335	59
336	59
337	55
338	51
339	47
340	42
341	42
357	81
358	81

400	
Block	Scale
402	208
402½	204
403	200
404	196
405	187
406	183
407	183
408	191
409	179
413	141
414	137
415	133
416	124
417	120
418	124
423	95
424	91
424½	95
425	86
426	82
427	80
428	78
429	75
430	74
431	69
432	66
433	66
434	61
435	61
436	59
437	51
438	51
439	42
440	32
441	32
442	28
445	74
455½	71
456	71
457	74
458	81
458½	81

500	
Block	Scale
501	212
502	204
503	204
504	200
507	187
508	183
509	175
510	183
513	154
514	162
516	133
517	128
518	120
519	116
520	112
521	107
522	95
523	91
524	91
525	82
526	80
527	78
528	75
529	72
530	71
531	68
532	65
533	59
534	57
534½	55
535	53
536	53
537	53
538	54
539	32
540	24
541	24
542	24
543	24
549	53
550	56
551	59
552	61
553	63
554	67
555	70
556	70
557	74
558	78
559	81

600	
Block	Scale
601	221
602	212
603	212
606	187
607	183
608	179
609	170
610	166
611	163
612	158
613	154
614	158
617	124
617½	120
618	120
618½	120
619	116
621	103
622	99
623	91
624	86
625	80
626	78
626½	82
627	75
627¼	75
627¾	78
628	72
629	70
630	66
631	63
632	59
633	55
634	47
635	49
636	40
637	41
638	40
639	24
640	20
641	Sub
642	Sub
643	Sub
646	36
647	40
648	44
649	47
650	50
651	53
652	59
653	63
654	65
655	67
656	69

700	
Block	Scale
702	226
703	225
704	225
705	204
710	162
711	158
711½	162
712	154
713	149
714	145
715	141
717	121
719	113
720	104
721	100
722	96
723	92
723½	95
724	87
724½	87
725	83
726	81
727	79
727½	79
728	73
728½	73
729	70
730	67
731	64
732	60
733	56
734	48
735	44
736	40
737	36
738	36
739	24
740	20
741	Sub
742	Sub
743	Sub
745	32
746	32
747	36
748	44
749	47
750	50
751	53
751½	56
752	59
753	61
754	63
755	65

800	
Block	Scale
803	217
804	221
805	200
807	179
810	162
811	158
812	149
813	145
814	145
815	137
815½	134
816	128
817	125
818	120
819	116
820	107
821	103
822	96
822½	95
823	92
823½	92
824	86
825	83
825¼	83
825¾	83
826	81
827	79
828	73
829	69
830	69
831	63
832	59
833	55
834	51
835	44
836	40
837	36
838	32
839	28
840	24
841	Sub
842	Sub
843	Sub
844	24
845	28
846	36
847	40
848	47
849	50
850	56
851	59
852	61
853	63
854	65
855	67
856	69

900	
Block	Scale
901	229
902	225
903	212
905	191
906	183
907	179
908	175
908½	175
909	166
910	162
911	162
911½	162
912	154
913	149
914	145
919	116
920	108
921	103
922	98
923	95
923½	95
924	91
924¼	90
924½	90
925	85
925¼	85
925½	85
926	80
926½	80
927	77
928	74
929	71
930	69
931	66
932	59
933	55
934	47
935	44
936	40
937	36
938	32
939	28
940	28
941	24
942	24
943	24
944	28
945	32
946	36
947	44
948	47
949	53
950	56
951	61
952	61
953	63

1000	
Block	Scale
1002	217
1003	205
1004	204
1005	191
1006	191
1007	183
1008	179
1010	175
1011	162
1013	158
1014	149
1015	145
1016	137
1017	133
1018	125
1019	117
1020	112
1021	107
1022	99
1023	95
1024	91
1024½	90
1025	85
1025½	86
1026	81
1026¼	81
1026½	81
1027	79
1027½	79
1028	74
1029	74
1030	68
1031	65
1032	62
1033	58
1034	50
1035	47
1036	44
1037	40
1038	36
1039	32
1040	32
1041	32
1042	32
1043	32
1044	36
1045	40
1046	44
1047	47
1048	53
1049	56
1050	59
1051	61

1100	
Block	Scale
1102	212
1103	208
1104	204
1105	208
1106	191
1107	196
1108	200
1112	166
1113	162
1114	158
1115	141
1116	140
1117	128
1118	124
1119	119
1120	111
1121	107
1122	102
1123	98
1124	94
1125	86
1126	81
1126¼	81
1126½	81
1127	79
1128	74
1129	72
1130	68
1131	68
1132	65
1133	59
1134	55
1134½	55
1135	50
1136	47
1137	44
1138	40
1139	40
1140	40
1141	37
1142	41
1143	36
1144	44
1145	47
1146	56
1147	59
1148	56
1149	63
1150	63
1151	63

1200	
Block	Scale
1203	209
1204	208
1205	211
1206	217
1207	204
1208	203
1211	175
1212	170
1217	137
1218	140
1218½	136
1219	120
1220	119
1221	111
1222	103
1223	98
1224	91
1224½	94
1225	85
1225¼	86
1225½	86
1226	81
1226½	85
1227	80
1228	78
1229	74
1230	71
1231	69
1232	66
1233	63
1233½	68
1234	59
1235	55
1236	50
1237	50
1238	47
1239	48
1240	44
1241	45
1242	49
1243	48
1244	50
1245	53
1246	56
1247	59
1248	61
1249	63
1250	63

1300	
Block	Scale
1303	217
1304	221
1305	208
1306	207
1307	204
1309	196
1310	183
1311	179
1313	161
1317	140
1319	127
1320	124
1321	115
1322	106
1323	99
1324	94
1324½	98
1325	95
1325½	95
1326	90
1326½	86
1327	82
1328	81
1329	77
1330	74
1331	72
1332	69
1333	71
1334	65
1335	58
1336	54
1337	57
1338	51
1339	55
1340	59
1341	53
1342	59
1343	59
1344	59
1345	59
1346	59
1347	65
1348	65
1349	66
1350	68

1400	
Block	Scale
1405	212
1406	199
1407	196
1408	191
1409	183
1410	188
1411	166
1412	162
1413	157
1414	153
1415	145
1416	141
1417	136
1418	128
1419	128
1420	120
1421	119
1422	107
1423	103
1424	102
1425	94
1425½	98
1426	94
1427	86
1428	82
1429	80
1430	78
1431	75
1432	77
1433	74
1433½	74
1434	65
1435	63
1436	63
1437	60
1438	58
1439	61
1440	59
1441	56
1442	56
1443	65
1444	65
1445	65
1446	65
1447	65
1448	67
1449	69

1500	
Block	Scale
1505	208
1506	204
1507	199
1508	187
1509	182
1510	178
1511	170
1511½	178
1513	162
1515	149
1518	128
1519	124
1520	116
1521	115
1521½	119
1522	111
1523	106
1524	106
1525	103
1525½	102
1526	99
1527	90
1528	85
1529	80
1530	80
1531	79
1532	74
1533	71
1534	68
1535	66
1536	66
1537	66
1538	64
1539	64
1540	63
1541	63
1542	71
1543	68
1544	68
1545	70
1546	68
1547	70
1548	70
1549	71

1600			
Block	Scale	Block	Scale
1607	200	1628	90
1608	196	1629	85
1609	191	1630	81
1610	187	1631	79
1611	186	1632	77
1612	170	1633	74
1613	170	1634	71
1614	170	1635	68
1615	161	1636	68
1617	153	1637	68
1618	145	1638	68
1619	128	1639	67
1620	123	1640	68
1621	120	1641	68
1622	116	1642	71
1623	115	1643	73
1624	111	1644	72
1625	106	1645	72
1625½	107	1646	72
1626	102	1647	72
1627	98		

1700			
Block	Scale	Block	Scale
1708	200	1728	94
1709	200	1729	91
1710	187	1730	85
1711	182	1731	81
1712	175	1732	81
1713	166	1733	79
1714	162	1734	75
1715	179	1735	73
1715½	161	1736	70
1716	149	1737	73
1717	145	1738	73
1718	141	1739	72
1719	137	1740	73
1720	127	1741	73
1721	124	1742	73
1723	119	1743	77
1724	119	1744	76
1724½	115	1745	76
1725	111	1746	74
1726	106		
1727	98		

1800			
Block	Scale	Block	Scale
1815	162	1835	74
1816	153	1836	74
1817	144	1837	74
1818	141	1838	77
1819	136	1839	74
1820	137	1840	75
1821	132	1841	75
1822	127	1842	77
1823	119	1843	77
1823½	123	1844	78
1824	119		
1825	115		
1826	106		
1827	106		
1828	98		
1829	98		
1830	90		
1831	85		
1832	85		
1833	81		
1834	76		

1900			
Block	Scale	Block	Scale
1921	140	1943	82
1922	136	1944	86
1923	136		
1926	111		
1927	106		
1927½	119		
1928	106		
1929	98		
1930	98		
1931	94		
1932	92		
1933	85		
1934	80		
1935	76		
1936	76		
1937	76		
1938	79		
1939	78		
1940	78		
1941	82		
1942	79		

2000	
Block	Scale
2024	132
2025	123
2026	115
2027	111
2028	111
2029	106
2030	98
2031	98
2031½	102
2032	98
2033	88
2034	88
2035	84
2036	87
2040	88
2041	86
2042	82
2043	86
2044	86
2045	93

2100	
Block	Scale
2125	123
2126	119
2127	115
2128	115
2129	111
2130	106
2143	93
2144	93
2145	93

2200	
Block	Scale
2226	123
2227	123
2228	119
2243	97
2244	97
2245	101

2300	
Block	Scale
2327	134
2328	127
2343	101
2344	105
2345	105

2400	
Block	Scale
2428	132
2445	111

2500	
Block	Scale
2544	123
2545	116

"Sub"—See Rate Table 2, page 4.

2/24/42.

RATE TABLE 2. BLOCK 742

SUB-BLOCK TARIFF.

To find the scale applicable between two sub-blocks, first ascertain from the Directory of Express Stations the sub-block letter of the originating station and the sub-block number and letter of the destination station. The number of the rate scale sought will be that number which is the intersection of the vertical column of figures beneath the letter of the sub-block of origin and the horizontal line of figures to the right of the number and letter of the sub-block of destination.

To— Blk.	Sub-bl.	From block 742, sub-block— A	B	C	D	E	F	G	H	I	K	L	M	N	O	P	Q
641	A	20	20	20	20	20	20	20	20	20	20	20	20	20	20	20	20
641	B	16	20	20	20	20	20	20	20	20	20	20	20	20	20	20	20
641	C	16	16	20	20	16	20	20	20	20	20	20	20	20	20	20	20
641	D	14	16	16	20	16	16	20	20	16	20	20	20	20	20	20	20
641	E	16	20	20	20	20	20	20	20	20	20	20	20	20	20	20	20
641	F	16	16	20	20	16	20	20	20	20	20	20	20	20	20	20	20
641	G	14	16	16	20	16	16	20	20	16	20	20	20	20	20	20	20
641	H	14	14	16	16	14	16	16	20	16	16	20	20	20	20	20	20
641	I	16	16	20	20	16	20	20	20	20	20	20	20	20	20	20	20
641	K	14	16	16	20	16	16	20	20	16	20	20	20	20	20	20	20
641	L	14	14	16	16	14	16	16	20	16	16	20	20	20	20	20	20
641	M	12	14	14	16	14	14	16	16	14	16	16	20	20	16	20	20
641	N	14	16	16	20	16	16	20	20	16	20	20	20	20	20	20	20
641	O	14	14	16	16	14	16	16	20	16	16	20	20	20	20	20	20
641	P	12	14	14	16	14	14	16	16	14	16	16	20	20	16	20	20
641	Q	11	12	14	14	12	14	14	16	14	14	16	16	16	16	16	20

To— Blk.	Sub-bl.	From block 742, sub-block— A	B	C	D	E	F	G	H	I	K	L	M	N	O	P	Q
642	A	14	14	16	16	14	16	16	20	16	16	20	20	20	20	20	20
642	B	..	..	..	..	..	..	..	..	..	..	..	..	..	..	..	..
642	C	16	16	16	14	16	16	16	16	20	20	20	16	20	20	20	20
642	D	16	16	16	16	20	20	20	16	20	20	20	20	20	20	20	20
642	E	12	14	14	16	14	14	16	16	14	16	16	20	20	16	20	20
642	F	14	14	14	14	14	14	14	16	16	16	16	16	20	16	16	20
642	G	14	14	14	14	16	16	16	14	16	16	16	16	20	20	20	16
642	H	16	14	14	12	16	16	14	14	20	16	16	14	20	20	16	16
642	I	11	12	14	14	12	14	14	16	14	14	16	16	16	16	16	20
642	K	12	12	12	14	14	14	14	14	14	14	14	16	16	16	16	16
642	L	14	12	12	12	14	14	14	14	16	14	14	14	16	16	16	16
642	M	14	14	12	11	16	14	14	12	16	16	14	14	20	16	16	14
642	N	10	11	14	16	11	12	14	14	12	14	14	16	16	14	16	16
642	O	11	10	11	12	12	11	12	14	14	12	14	14	14	14	14	16
642	P	12	11	10	11	14	12	11	12	14	14	14	14	16	14	14	14
642	Q	14	12	11	10	14	14	12	11	16	14	14	12	16	16	14	14

To— Blk.	Sub-bl.	From block 742, sub-block— A	B	C	D	E	F	G	H	I	K	L	M	N	O	P	Q
643	A	20	20	20	16	20	20	20	20	20	20	20	20	20	20	20	20
643	B	20	20	20	20	20	20	20	16	20	20	20	20	20	20	20	20
643	C	..	..	..	..	..	..	..	..	..	..	..	..	..	..	..	..
643	D	..	..	..	..	..	..	..	..	..	..	..	..	..	..	..	..
643	E	20	20	20	20	20	20	20	20	20	20	20	20	20	20	20	20
643	F	20	16	20	20	20	20	20	20	20	20	20	20	20	20	20	20
643	G	..	..	..	..	..	..	..	..	..	..	..	..	..	..	..	..
643	H	..	..	..	..	..	..	..	..	..	..	..	..	..	..	..	..
643	I	20	20	20	20	20	20	20	20	20	20	20	20	20	20	20	20
643	K	20	20	20	20	20	20	20	20	20	20	20	20	20	20	20	20
643	L	..	..	..	..	..	..	..	..	..	..	..	..	..	..	..	..
643	M	..	..	..	..	..	..	..	..	..	..	..	..	..	..	..	..
643	N	16	16	14	14	20	16	16	14	20	20	16	16	20	20	20	16
643	O	20	20	16	16	20	20	16	16	20	20	20	16	20	20	20	20
643	P	20	20	16	14	20	16	16	14	20	20	16	16	20	20	20	16
643	Q	..	..	..	..	..	..	..	..	..	..	..	..	..	..	..	..

To— Blk.	Sub-bl.	From block 742, sub-block— A	B	C	D	E	F	G	H	I	K	L	M	N	O	P	Q
741	A	16	16	20	20	14	20	20	20	16	16	20	20	16	20	20	20
741	B	14	16	20	20	14	16	20	20	16	16	16	20	16	16	20	20
741	C	11	12	16	16	12	14	14	16	14	14	16	16	16	16	16	20
741	D	10	11	14	16	11	12	14	14	14	14	14	16	16	14	16	16
741	E	14	16	20	20	14	16	20	20	16	16	16	20	16	16	20	20
741	F	14	14	20	20	12	16	16	20	14	14	16	16	14	16	16	20
741	G	12	14	16	20	11	14	16	16	12	14	14	16	14	14	16	16
741	H	11	12	16	16	10	14	14	16	12	12	14	14	14	14	14	16
741	I	16	20	20	20	16	20	20	20	16	16	20	20	14	16	16	20
741	K	14	16	20	20	14	16	16	20	14	14	16	16	14	14	16	16
741	L	14	16	16	20	14	14	16	16	12	14	14	16	12	14	14	16
741	M	14	14	14	16	12	12	14	14	10	11	12	14	14	12	14	14
741	N	16	20	20	20	16	16	20	20	14	16	16	20	14	14	16	16
741	O	16	16	20	20	14	16	16	20	14	14	16	16	12	14	14	16
741	P	14	16	16	20	14	14	16	16	12	14	14	16	11	12	14	14
741	Q	16	16	16	20	14	14	16	16	14	12	14	14	10	11	12	14

To— Blk.	Sub-bl.	From block 742, sub-block— A	B	C	D	E	F	G	H	I	K	L	M	N	O	P	Q
742	A	9	10	14	14	10	11	12	14	12	12	14	14	14	14	14	16
742	B	10	9	12	14	11	10	11	12	12	12	12	14	14	14	14	14
742	C	14	12	9	10	14	11	10	11	14	14	12	12	16	14	14	14
742	D	14	14	10	9	16	14	11	11	14	14	14	12	16	16	14	14
742	E	10	11	14	16	9	11	14	14	11	11	12	14	14	12	14	14
742	F	11	10	11	14	11	9	10	11	11	11	11	12	14	12	12	14
742	G	12	11	10	11	14	10	9	10	12	12	11	11	14	14	12	12
742	H	14	12	11	11	14	11	10	9	14	12	11	10	14	14	12	11
742	I	12	12	14	14	11	11	12	14	9	10	11	12	12	11	12	14
742	K	12	12	14	14	11	11	12	12	10	9	10	11	11	10	11	12
742	L	14	12	12	14	12	11	11	11	11	10	9	10	12	11	10	11
742	M	14	14	12	12	14	12	11	10	12	11	10	9	14	12	11	10
742	N	14	14	16	16	14	14	14	16	12	12	14	14	9	10	11	12
742	O	14	14	14	16	12	12	14	14	11	10	11	12	10	9	10	11
742	P	14	14	14	14	14	12	12	12	12	11	10	11	11	10	9	10
742	Q	16	14	14	14	14	14	12	11	14	12	11	10	12	11	10	9

To— Blk.	Sub-bl.	From block 742, sub-block— A	B	C	D	E	F	G	H	I	K	L	M	N	O	P	Q
743	A	16	16	14	14	20	16	16	14	16	16	14	14	20	16	16	14
743	B	16	16	14	14	20	16	16	14	16	16	14	14	20	16	16	14
743	C	20	16	16	14	20	20	16	16	20	16	16	14	20	20	16	16
743	D	..	..	..	..	..	..	..	..	..	..	..	..	..	..	..	..
743	E	16	16	14	14	16	14	14	12	14	14	12	11	16	14	14	12
743	F	20	16	16	16	16	16	14	14	16	14	14	12	16	16	14	14
743	G	..	..	..	..	..	..	..	..	..	..	..	..	..	..	..	..
743	H	..	..	..	..	..	..	..	..	..	..	..	..	..	..	..	..
743	I	16	14	14	14	14	14	12	11	14	12	11	10	14	14	12	11
743	K	..	..	..	..	..	..	..	..	..	..	..	..	..	..	..	..
743	L	..	..	..	..	..	..	..	..	..	..	..	..	..	..	..	..
743	M	..	..	..	..	..	..	..	..	..	..	..	..	..	..	..	..
743	N	..	..	..	..	..	..	..	..	..	..	..	..	..	..	..	..
743	O	..	..	..	..	..	..	..	..	..	..	..	..	..	..	..	..
743	P	..	..	..	..	..	..	..	..	..	..	..	..	..	..	..	..
743	Q	..	..	..	..	..	..	..	..	..	..	..	..	..	..	..	..

To— Blk.	Sub-bl.	From block 742, sub-block— A	B	C	D	E	F	G	H	I	K	L	M	N	O	P	Q
841	A	20	20	20	20	16	20	20	20	16	16	20	20	14	16	16	20
841	B	16	20	20	20	16	16	20	20	14	16	16	20	14	14	16	16
841	C	16	16	20	20	14	16	16	20	14	14	16	16	12	14	14	16
841	D	16	16	20	20	16	16	16	16	14	14	14	16	11	12	14	14
841	E	20	20	20	20	20	20	20	20	16	20	20	20	16	16	20	20
841	F	20	20	20	20	16	20	20	20	16	16	20	20	14	16	16	20
841	G	16	20	20	20	16	16	20	20	14	16	16	20	14	14	16	16
841	H	20	20	20	20	16	16	20	20	16	14	16	16	12	14	14	16
841	I	20	20	20	20	20	20	20	20	20	20	20	20	16	20	20	20
841	K	20	20	20	20	20	20	20	20	16	20	20	20	16	16	20	20
841	L	20	20	20	20	20	20	20	20	20	16	20	20	14	16	16	20
841	M	20	20	20	20	20	20	20	20	16	16	16	20	14	14	16	16
841	N	20	20	20	20	20	20	20	20	20	20	20	20	20	20	20	20
841	O	20	20	20	20	20	20	20	20	20	20	20	20	16	20	20	20
841	P	20	20	20	20	20	20	20	20	20	20	20	20	16	16	20	20
841	Q	20	20	20	20	20	20	20	20	20	16	20	20	14	16	16	20

To— Blk.	Sub-bl.	From block 742, sub-block— A	B	C	D	E	F	G	H	I	K	L	M	N	O	P	Q
842	A	16	16	16	20	14	14	16	16	14	12	14	14	10	11	12	14
842	B	14	14	16	16	14	14	14	14	12	11	12	14	11	10	11	12
842	C	16	14	14	16	14	14	14	14	14	12	11	12	12	11	10	11
842	D	..	..	..	..	..	..	..	..	..	..	..	..	..	..	..	..
842	E	16	16	20	20	16	16	16	16	14	14	14	16	14	12	14	14
842	F	16	16	16	20	14	14	16	16	14	12	14	14	12	11	12	14
842	G	16	16	20	20	16	16	16	16	14	14	14	16	14	12	14	14
842	H	20	20	20	20	16	16	20	20	16	14	16	16	14	14	14	16
842	I	20	20	20	20	16	16	20	20	16	14	16	16	14	14	14	16
842	K	16	16	20	20	16	16	16	16	14	14	14	16	14	12	14	14
842	L	20	20	20	20	16	16	20	20	16	14	16	16	14	14	14	16
842	M	20	20	20	20	20	20	20	20	16	16	16	20	16	14	16	16
842	N	20	20	20	20	20	20	20	20	16	16	16	20	16	14	16	16
842	O	20	20	20	20	16	16	20	20	16	14	16	16	14	14	14	16
842	P	20	20	20	20	20	20	20	20	16	16	16	20	16	14	16	16
842	Q	20	20	20	20	20	20	20	20	20	16	20	20	16	16	16	20

To— Blk.	Sub-bl.	From block 742, sub block— A	B	C	D	E	F	G	H	I	K	L	M	N	O	P	Q
843	A	..	..	..	..	..	..	..	..	..	..	..	..	..	..	..	..
843	B	..	..	..	..	..	..	..	..	..	..	..	..	..	..	..	..
843	C	..	..	..	..	..	..	..	..	..	..	..	..	..	..	..	..
843	D	..	..	..	..	..	..	..	..	..	..	..	..	..	..	..	..
843	E	20	20	20	20	20	20	20	20	16	16	16	20	16	14	16	16
843	F	20	20	20	20	20	20	20	20	20	20	20	20	20	16	20	20
843	G	..	..	..	..	..	..	..	..	..	..	..	..	..	..	..	..
843	H	..	..	..	..	..	..	..	..	..	..	..	..	..	..	..	..
843	I	20	20	20	20	20	20	20	20	20	16	20	20	16	16	16	20
843	K	20	20	20	20	20	20	20	20	20	20	20	20	20	16	20	20
843	L	20	20	20	20	20	20	20	20	20	20	20	20	20	20	20	20
843	M	20	20	20	24	20	20	20	20	20	20	20	20	20	20	20	20
843	N	20	20	20	20	20	20	20	20	20	20	20	20	20	16	20	20
843	O	20	20	20	20	20	20	20	20	20	20	20	20	20	20	20	20
843	P	20	20	20	24	20	20	20	20	20	20	20	20	20	20	20	20
843	Q	20	20	24	24	20	20	20	20	20	20	20	20	20	20	20	20

32. No employee is authorized, but, on the contrary, prohibited from contracting any debts, making or accepting drafts, or making notes, due-bills, or other money obligations or accounts against the Company. Agents are not authorized to buy or contract for any fixtures or personal property, unless they have received permission from the Superintendent; and for every expenditure exceeding $5.00 in amount, *special* permission for that particular expenditure must be obtained from him. In all cases where a purchase is made, a bill and duplicate properly receipted should be taken, the *original* to be used as a voucher, and the duplicate to be placed on file in the office where the money was paid out. Vouchers for all expenses must be sent to Buffalo. They can always be sent in payment of amounts due on statements, but are liable to be returned if not approved.

33. Agents, exclusively engaged to attend to the Company's business, will not absent themselves from the same without permission from the Superintendent of their Division.

34. Agents will be held responsible for loss arising from their own carelessness, inattention, or want of prudence; or such proportion of loss as may be determined by the Superintendent. No office should be left a moment unless in charge of a regular watch, or some person in the employ of the Company. Ordinary door locks are not the slightest protection. A burglar will walk in with his false keys in less time than an honest man would with the real ones. The employees of the Company are watched by *skillful and desperate thieves*, who will take advantage of the slightest oversight or carelessness.

35. A judicious use should be made of the "franking privilege." All packages franked at an office should bear

the signature of the Agent. When a package is entered free on a way-bill, give the address of the consignor. When packages are entered on way-bill to collect , and the Agent delivering franks the same, he should in all cases state on way-bill the cause of its being made free.

36. Report any misconduct on the part of Messengers, such as drinking intoxicating liquor while on duty, carrying money packages past way-stations, leaving their safes unguarded, &c., to the Superintendent of their Division. *When the Messengers leave their cars at a station for meals, the Agent will either remain in charge of it, or substitute a suitable person.*

37. Make a judicious use of the privileges granted to us by the telegraph companies. Avail yourself of them only when our interests demand it, and avoid superfluous words. Never use the lines at the request of other parties, unless the telegraph charges are paid by them.

GENERAL INSTRUCTIONS TO MESSENGERS.

1. The following instructions are made to secure the Company and Messengers against loss. They must be strictly observed, and *will be rigidly enforced.*

2. You will in all cases be required to give a bond for the faithful performance of duties; you must obey all orders of the Superintendent of your Division, and at the end of your route will be at the disposal of the Agent. You must report yourself ready for duty in ample time to transact business without haste or confusion. You must

know that you get all packages entered upon your way-bills, and as soon as you arrive at the end of your route, check to the Agent or clerk, to relieve you of responsibility. When packages are short, or in bad order, so note it on the way-bill and give reasons, if known, signing your name to it.

3. Taking a way-bill from an office or a messenger, upon which goods are short, without having a memorandum to that effect made on it before receiving, will be presumptive evidence that you had all the bill called for.

4. Every way-bill carried by you must have your name entered thereon, and your initials or check-mark opposite each entry, and all bills delivered to Agents or others, *en route*, must show your *out* check-mark as evidence that the package was left with the way-bill. Blank books are provided, in which all way-bills carried by you *must* be entered, and on which you will take the receipt of the person to whom you deliver the same. Always leave memorandum way-bills with packages delivered to non-reporting Agents.

5. In receiving fruit or vegetables, you must see that each package is in good order, and you will be held accountable for its safe keeping while in your possession; and, in all cases, will refuse to receive from other parties in bad condition, *except* the party delivering, note on the way-bill accordingly, signing his name to such notation. A neglect to have this done, will hold you liable for all damages on such shipment.

6. Books are also provided in which you will take receipts for matter delivered to non-reporting Agents, or other persons. Great care must be taken in delivering such matter to strangers; always require them to

be identified by some person that you know, and note the name of the person identifying on your receipt book, under the entry.

7. Money must invariably be carried to and from the office and cars, in your safe; and while so carried must be constantly in sight—when possible, within *reach*. Specie must never be carried outside of safe, when it can be put in it. *The carring of money in carpet bags, outside of safes, no matter how short the distance, is positively forbidden.*

8. When an accident occurs to your train, that is likely to prevent you from making connections with other roads, telegraph at the first opportunity to the Agent at the connecting point, stating facts briefly. If the accident endangers your safe, or goods, telegraph the nearest office that can render you assistance. Guard your car carefully against *fire;* should a fire occur, *secure your safe the first thing*, and next the packages. If necessary, cut away the car, and sacrifice other goods to get out your safe.

9. When you have a separate car, or apartment for your exclusive use, do not allow any person to ride therein, except by consent of the Superintendent. *You must not leave your safe on the route, except at meal time*, when the Agent at that point will remain in charge of it. Any deviation from this rule, except by the *written permission* of the Superintendent, or his assistants, will cause your immediate dismissal. Before going to your meals, examine your safe and see that it is locked, and observe the condition of its contents. On returning, re-examine to see if its contents have been disturbed. Never leave it *open, or unlocked*, one moment longer than is absolutely necessary, even when you are entirely alone. Always test the locking by lifting at the lid, after *removing the key*. *When express goods are carried in freight cars*, and

you are authorized by the Superintendent to ride in another part of the train, examine the condition of them at *every stopping place.*

10. Show proper respect to all persons, and particularly those connected with the route on which you are running.

11. Handle goods with care, and have them properly stowed for safe carriage. *No article,* of whatever description, must be *thrown, dropped, or allowed to fall,* no matter how short the distance. The "ending over" of boxes, throwing or rolling of trunks, bales, &c., will not be tolerated. If goods are injured by accident while in your charge, note it on the way-bill, and report the same to the Superintendent.

12. Messengers will be held responsible for loss or damage from carrying packages or freight past the proper office for transfer, or past destination, unless for good reasons.

13. Paste one of your route labels securely on every package and article billed by you.

14. Refuse money packages unless properly sealed—(see instructions to Agents in reference to seals,) and under no circumstance, sign any but the regular printed form of receipt, used by the Company.

15. When on cars, or boats, you will be subject to the rules for employees of the road, or boat, upon which you are traveling.

16. *You are positively prohibited* from drinking intoxicating liquor, of any kind, while on duty. Never receive from strangers, cigars, tobacco, or anything else that can be drugged. Never show or talk about the contents of your safe. Take note of any suspicious

character you discover lurking around watching your car. Take great care of your safe keys, and never let them go out of your possession, except to some one authorized to receive them. Carelessness, which would enable thieves to obtain a wax impression of your key, and thereby rob you, would tend to criminate yourselves.

17. You will not be permitted to change off, or leave your regular "run," without permission from the Superintendent of your Division.

18. You are positively forbidden to *speculate* in any way, shape or manner, and if found so doing, *will be discharged.*

19. When goods are way-billed to the wrong office, make a duplicate of the original bill, to the office whither they should have been sent; noting on the original, "duplicate same number and date made to (*here insert name of office.*)" and forward the original way-bill to the office for which it was intended, and the goods, with duplicate, to destination. *Never change the destination of a way-bill by altering the heading.*

20. When you have goods on a memorandum bill, copy the bill in full, on your way-bill register, taking receipt in the usual form. All matter carried by you without bills, must either be regularly billed by you, or else entered upon your way-bill register, making memorandum bill for same, so that you will be prepared to answer any inquiries as to lost or delayed goods.

21. You must provide yourself with a copy of this tariff, which will give the rate to all points, from the office at each end of your route. In making charges on matter received and billed by you, from intermediate points on your route, to other points or beyond, you will divide the rate for whole length of your route, and charge on same

according to the distance the package is to be carried, and if the same is destined to a point beyond your route, add the rate given from office at end of your route to destination of package, or to office for which you make the way-bill. All circulars in reference to new offices or other matters, and all special tariffs, received by you, must be preserved for reference, and fastened in back of this tariff.

22. You will also keep yourself supplied with the stamps required by Government, under the national tax law, using same (as per instructions to Agents, to which you will refer,) on all matter billed by you, except that delivered by non-reporting offices.

23. You are required to report each trip, (to such office as the Superintendent may designate,) all weights on *regular* Way-Bills carried by you, according to the form of blank freight report furnished for that purpose. When the weight is not given on the Way-Bill, you will estimate and report the same as near as possible. All packages of twenty pounds and upwards must be reported. When your route extends over more than one line of Railroad, you will make separate reports for each road.

24. When extraordinary circumstances make it seem advisable to vary from any of the foregoing rules, consult the Superintendent and get his written consent thereto.

GENERAL AND SPECIAL INSTRUCTIONS TO NON-REPORTING AGENTS.

1. Non-Reporting Agents will follow the instructions given by the Division Superintendents.

2. All packages received by you for delivery, must be delivered at once, if the consignee is known and within reasonable distance—if not, a notice through the post office must be given without delay.

3. On receipt of packages, or other matter, from Messengers, you will advance the charges on the same, and enter upon your book, taking receipt of the party to whom they are delivered; if delivered to any other person than the one addressed, it must be only upon the written order of that party, which order must be attached to your report when forwarded to the general office for payment of commissions.

4. Messengers are required to deliver you, with all matter left, a memorandum Way-Bill, which is a duplicate of the receipt given by you to them, and must be compared with the packages, at once, to see that it is correct. This, if possible, you must do before the messenger leaves the station, so that you can call his immediate attention to any error, and request him to correct it. Where there is not time to check the matter with the Way-Bill before the train leaves, you must do so as soon as possible thereafter; and if anything is wrong, notify the Messenger at once by telegraph, or by writing if there is no telegraph at your station. You will also call the Messenger's attention to the fact upon his return trip. Failing to give such notice to Messengers, you will be held as having received the matter as per Way-Bill.

5. If packages or collections left with you, remain on hand one week uncalled for, or unpaid, you will return them with the duplicate bill, to the Messenger from whom you received the same, (or if he has left the route, to some other Messenger) who will refund the charges you advanced, and bill the same to the nearest regular office. If such packages are called for afterwards, you can order them returned.

6. The memorandum way-bill left with you by Messenger, must be preserved and forwarded with your monthly statement.

7. *No commission will be allowed upon business, except a receipt for same is shown, it is therefore necessary that you should be very particular in this respect—also to date the Book for each day's business.* No commissions are allowed *when* goods are returned to the Messenger.

8. *Commissions are allowed only on the item of our charges collected and prepaid, at your office;* not on collections of bills of purchase, drafts, or accounts, nor upon advanced charges to other parties, nor prepaid charges on matter delivered to you.

9. All entries of matter *not delivered* at the time you render the monthly statement, must be erased from it, and opposite such entry write " Package on hand," entering the same on the following month's report.

10. On receipt of a package to be forwarded, you will at once make the proper entry upon your book, and deliver to the first Messenger passing in the direction that the package is destined, taking his receipt, and paying over to him the charges, *if prepaid by shipper.*

11. Require persons forwarding money or valuable

packages to put them up and *direct them*—sealing with their own seal if they have one, but should you seal them, let it be in their presence, and under no circumstances, must you put the address on such packages.

12. Unless you have a safe, and some one sleeping near it, you must decline receiving packages of money that you will have to hold over night, unless it is impossible for parties to deliver to you before Messenger passes the next day. If you have no safe, do not leave money or valuable packages in a desk or drawer, but keep them in your pocket, or some safe place not in your office. We want you to hold packages in your possession as short time as possible, and during that time *take care of them.*

13. On application to the principal office in the Division, all stationery, necessary for the transaction of the business, will be furnished you.

For instructions as to the business generally, and in reference to collections in particular, see "general instructions," to regular agents.

SPECIAL INSTRUCTIONS TO AGENTS.

WAY-BILLS.

Number, date and time of Bills

All Bills issued by you in any one day bear the same number, and when more than one bill is made to the same office on the same day, the time of departure, A. M. or P. M., should be entered on each, and so Abstracted.

Commence new numbers.

On the first of January each year, commence at Number One (1) and continue numbering without regard to dates, advancing one number each day that you forward one or more bills.

Make Bills direct to,

You can make bills direct to all *regular offices* west of Buffalo. But for places east of that, (unless otherwise directed herein) you will bill to Buffalo or Suspension Bridge.

Make Bills for way business.

Matter for way or non-reporting offices, you will bill to end of route in the direction same may be going.

Make Way-Bills and charges for business beyond our route.

For any point off our lines you will only make Way-Bills and charges to the office to which such article is billed by you. But, if the charges are prepaid to destination, extend the full amount paid, in prepaid column, adding in column of "Remarks" "Paid through." This rule also applies to matter upon which charges have been "agreed through;" enter charges only to points billed, and note in column of "Remarks" the rate

Special agreements. agreed. All special agreements must be noted on the Way-Bill. Matter for points off our lines, or which must pass through the hands of other Express Companies before reaching destination, must be billed to the Transfer Office nearest to destination. Such offices Transfer offices. are designated in tariff by being printed in large capitals, thus—CHICAGO.

Places of same name in same & different States. NOTE. Great care should be taken in making bills and abstracts for places of same names in different States—for instance, Decatur, Mich. and Ill.; Geneva, Ohio, Wis. and Ill.; London, Ohio and C. W.; Peru, Ind and Ill.; Paris, Ill. and C. W.; Galesburg, Ill. and Mich.; Hamilton, C. W. and Ohio; Madison, Ohio and Wis.; Springfield, Pa., Ill. and Ohio; Marshall, Iowa and Mich.; Quincy, Ind. and Ill., always enter the name of the State upon the Bill and Abstract.

Copy Bills forwarded, You wll keep correct copies ot all bills forwarded by you in a book provided for that purpose.

Make a price for each entry upon your way bill according to tariff furnished, unless it is a "Free," "S C" or "P O R" package.

Charges and season contracts. In forwarding bank notes under season contract ("S. C."), you will enter on way-bill in column "from whom received," the parties names under whose contract package is forwarded.

In no instance must you bill a package "S. C." *to account* of Consignee, *even if package is so marked*, unless you are so instructed by the Superintendent.

ABSTRACTS.

Abstracts of business forwarded from your office must give the number, date, place to, and the total footing of each Way-Bill, and also total footing of your trip book. Each Way-Bill issued by your office, must be abstracted, whether the same be "FREE," "P. O. R.," or "S. C."

Form of abstracts.

Abstracts must be returned to the General Office at Buffalo, weekly, or oftener when specially instructed. The last abstract in each month should end with the bills forwarded on the last day of the month.

When to be rendered,

All prepaid, or advanced charges on your abstracts, must be settled in the first statements of Way-Bills returned, after the abstract is made. Agents will return Messenger Abstracts in same manner as their own, except entering name of *Messenger* instead of office.

When to be settled.

STATEMENTS.

Statements give the place from, and to, the number, date and total footing of each Way-Bill received by you, with deductions on same, and are numbered as returned, (using but one number for a statement,) commencing at number one, January first of each year. Offices whose receipts are less than $500 per month, will report twice a month; $500 to 1,000, weekly; $1,000 to $2,500, tri-weekly; $2,500 and upwards, daily.

Statements number, form

When to be rendered.

Deductions, or Refunded.

Explain alterations on Way-Bill.

In entering the Way-Bills on statement, if any deductions are made, you will enter the total amount of same on each Way-Bill, in the "deduction" column. Always note any alteration of charges on Way-Bill, giving reasons in full for the same, as to whether it be "overcharged," "should be free," "S. C." or "P. O. R." After entering all bills to be returned, deduct the total amount of deductions, from total amount of bills, then add the amount due on abstracts, by *giving the number of first and last Way-Bill entered* on same, and if the abstract of a Messenger, enter Messenger's name also. To settle the statement credit yourself with the advanced charges, if any, on the same abstracts, paying balance with vouchers, and cash.

Settlement of Statements.

To whom sent.

The Statement, Way-Bills, vouchers and cash, are all to be done up in one package, and addressed "Livingston, Fargo & Co., Buffalo," marking on the outside the amount of cash only, Arrange the Way-Bills in the order in which they are entered on your statement, and fold each separately, over the tin form furnished you for that purpose.

Arrangement and folding Way-Bills.

Retaining Way-Bills to balance packages on hand

Unless you are provided with a bank for the purpose, you will retain a sufficient amount of Way-Bills of *last dates*, to cover the charges on all goods remaining on hand *at* the time of making the statement.

Retain copies of Statements.

Copies of Way-Bills received, and also statements forwarded, must be kept in books furnished for that purpose.

COLLECTIONS.

Collections with or without goods.

Too much care cannot be given to the collection of endorsed drafts, notes and bills; also of bills sent with goods, (C. O. D.) to collect on delivery.

Observe instructions on envelopes.

The printed instructions on the collection envelopes, and all special instructions, written thereon, must be strictly followed.

You should use sound discretion with regard to the kind of money you take on collections.

Kind of money to be taken.

The custom of the place where the collection is made, determines the kind of money in which it is to be paid, unless the face of the paper specifies it.

As far as possible, collect in such funds as will best suit the party for whom the collection is made.

When draft is returned in payment.

Where instructions are given to return proceeds of collection by draft, have the draft made payable to the order of the party in whose favor the collection is made. *Never to the order of the Express Company.*

When instructed as to kind of funds to return.

Directions to "return proceeds in specie," or "exchange," authorize the agent to sell such money as he may properly receive, and buy gold, silver or draft, noting expense of the same, on the envelope.

Receipt to be given.

When drafts, notes or bills are taken for collection, always give the Company's collection receipt. Enclose the paper for collection in the proper collection envelope, entering on same the name and address of the party from whom received, and of whom to be collected, and under the head of "special instructions," give such directions as you may receive from the sender, and if to be protested, write in full and plainly across the envelope, "*Protest if not paid.*" When instructions to protest are given, the place of *residence* of the endorser should be written on the draft, or note, under their names.

Form of forwarding collections.

When to be protested give residence of parties liable.

When bills are taken, accompanying goods, to be collected on delivery of same, enclose them in the printed "C. O. D." envelope for that purpose, and mark plainly on package "C. O. D.," *and also amount of bill to be collected.*

Goods with "C. O. D."

Avoid superfluous instructions on collection envelopes, and be careful that the special instructions given do not conflict with any stipulation on the face of the paper taken for collection.

Instructions must not conflict.

Goods marked "C. O. D." must only be delivered, or suffered to go out of your possession, on payment of the full amount of the bill which accompanies them. You will not *forward* them until our charges and collection are paid, nor return them without a written order from shipper. *Preserve the order.*

Delivering and returning "C. O. D." packages.

You must not deliver a portion of the goods on payment of a like portion of the

Agents must not allow "C. O. D." packages to be opened.

bill, unless by special instructions in writing from the shipper. When "C. O. D." goods arrive in advance of, or without the collection, immediately notify the office from whence they were sent, giving the name of consignee and consignor, if known. You may deliver the goods, if satisfied of the proper amount to collect, and remit the same at once, to the office from whence the goods were received, giving such information as will enable the agent at that point to deliver the money to the proper owner.

When goods and "C. O. D." get separated, how to proceed.

Under ordinary circumstances (or without instructions to the contrary) we consider the holding of notes, drafts or accounts one week after first presentation, a sufficient length of time, after which you will return the same, stating reasons for non-payment. Where parties are unknown, inquiry must be made without delay, from the office sending the collection; if the party cannot be found, return the same, after holding one week, with proper explanation for so doing. Collections with goods, if not called for, you will hold one week before making inquiry, at expiration of which time, you will ask instructions from office shipping as to what disposition shall be made of the same. When goods are refused, or left on your hands, for other reasons than herein provided, immediate notice must be given office shipping the same.

Proper length of time to hold collections when not paid.

At the last session of the Legislature in the state of Illinois, an act was passed providing for uniformity in calculating days of

Special law of the State of Illinais in reference to Bills of Exchange.

grace, maturity, of bills &c., which reads as follows:

"AN ACT *to provide for uniformity in calculating days of grace, maturity of bills, &c., and declaratory of the law in relation thereto.*

"SECTION 1. Be it enacted, by the people of the State of Illinois, represented in General Assembly: That no promissory note, check, draft, bill of exchange, order, or other negotiable or commercial instrument, payable at sight or on demand, or on presentment, shall be entitled to day of grace, but shall be absolutely payable on presentment. All other bills of exchange, drafts, or promissory notes, shall be entitled to the usual days of grace."

All paper payable at sight not entitled to days of grace.

Legal Holidays.

SECTION 2. The following days, *to-wit*: "The first day of January, commonly called New Years' day, the fourth day of July, and the "twenty-fifth day of December, commonly called Christmas day, and any appointed or recommended by the Governor of this State, or the President of the United States, as a day of fast or thanksgiving, shall, for all purposes whatsoever, as regards the presenting for payment or acceptance, the maturity and protesting, and giving notice of the dishonor of bills of exchange, bank checks and promissory notes, or other negotiable or commercial paper or instruments, be treated and considered as in the first day of the week, commonly called Sunday, and all notes, bills, "drafts, checks, or other evidence of indebt-"edness, falling due or maturing on either of "said days, shall be deemed as due, or hav-"ing matured the day previous; and should "two or three of those days come together, "or immediately succeeding each other, then "such instrument, paper or indebtedness, "shall be deemed as due, or having matured "on the day previous, to the first of such "days.

Paper falling due such day payable the day previous.

"SECTION 3. In computation of time and "of interest or discount, when the calculation "is by days or months, *thirty days shall be a* "*month*, but a year shall be twelve calendar "months; and interest for any number of "days less than a month, shall be estimated "by the proportion such number of days "shall bear to thirty.

Time paper to be calculated at *thirty days* to the month.

"SECTION 4. This act shall be in force "and take effect from and after its passage.

"Approved Feb. 22, 1861."

All commercial paper made or payable in the State of Illinois, since this act was passed, will mature in conformity with the provisions of same, and if so ordered, must be protested when due, *without reference to the place where it may be made or endorsed.*

In order to insure the return to us of all collections passing out of our hands to other companies, and also that we may have less trouble in keeping our accounts of such business, agents at transfer offices will, in each and every instance hereafter, *re-envelope all collections transferred to other companies,*

Collections passing into hands of other Companies, how transferred.

retaining the original envelope in their possession until the return of collection.

In filling out the new envelope, you will make it in favor of "American Express Co." at your office, and be *very particular* to enter thereon all special or general instructions given on the original envelope.

When such collections are returned to you, you will enclose the same in the original envelope, *without breaking the seal of the company returning it*, and again seal, with your seal, in the usual way.

Agents are required to rebill returned collections to the office from whence they were billed, except collections from Suspension Bridge office, (originating east of that point) which must be rebilled to Buffalo.

A book is furnished each regular office, in which all collections made or forwarded, must be entered, as per form therein. For the further information of agents, in making collections, the following remarks are subjoined.

ACCEPTANCE OF A BILL OR DRAFT.

Manner of accepting Drafts, &c.

An acceptance is an engagement to pay a bill or draft, and is done by the drawee (the person on whom the draft is made) writing "accepted" across the face of the paper, and subscribing his name, and when a specified time of payment is mentioned, (as ten days after sight) the drawee should date the time cf acceptance.

When instructions are to protest for non-payment, or non-acceptance, and it is not paid or accepted, it must be protested, or the endorsers are discharged from liability.

Protest if not paid or accepted.

A draft must be presented for payment and properly protested on the day it becomes due, or the Express Company will be held liable for its payment, and the endorser exonerated. Even the bankruptcy, insolvency, or death of the acceptor, (or drawee), will not excuse a neglect to demand payment of the assignees or executors, nor will the insufficiency of a draft or note, in any respect, constitute an excuse, so far as we are concerned, for non-payment. The presentment should be made at a reasonable time of day, when the bill is due.

Must be protested when due.

Time of presenting.

If the paper be made payable at any specified place, it must be presented at such place for payment.

Presented where payable.

If a draft or note fall due on Sunday, or any public holiday, and if such holiday fall on Monday, the paper becomes due on Saturday, except in States where, by law, it becomes due the *day after*, Sunday or holiday.

When due on Sunday or any other public holiday.

Due diligence must be used in presenting any description of bill or paper for acceptance.

When any doubt arises as to the proper course to pursue in making a collection, always consult a lawyer, bank officer, or some one competent to advise.

Doubtful cases obtain advice.

SPECIAL INSTRUCTIONS TO MESSENGERS.

WAY BILLS.

You will make and number bills same as an office. You are not expected to be cognizant of any season contract, (S. C.), and will make regular charges on every package, unless specially instructed to the contrary.

ABSTRACTS.

Abstracts must be made (same form as office) weekly, or oftener, if so instructed; presenting same with your trip book, for examination and settlement, to the cashier or agent at such office as the superintendent may designate, taking receipt thereon from party with whom settlement is made, for all moneys paid over.

Temporary messengers will use the abstract blanks printed for that purpose.

Billing packages to way stations.

All matter for non-reporting offices, or for way-points, where we have no agent, must be billed at the office at the end of the route, in the direction the package may be going.

American Express Company.

SPECIAL RATES AND INSTRUCTIONS.

GOLD TARIFF—Where the rate on bank notes is *less than one dollar*, add 25 cents per $1,000 for gold; where rate is one dollar or over, add 50 cents per $1,000.

SILVER TARIFF—Charge double the gold rate for silver.

COLLECTION TARIFF.

NOTES, DRAFTS AND ACCOUNTS.—For the collection of notes, drafts and accounts, *charge double* the rate on bank note packages of same amount.

GOODS.—For the collection of invoices with goods, ("C. O. D.,") of amounts less than $25.00, charge ordinary package rates; over that amount charge *one-half* more than for bank note packages of same amount. Collections of all kinds made by other companies, will only be charged *at package rates* by this company. The same will also apply to collections made by this company, and rebilled from one division to another, the division making the collection will charge the collection rate, all others the package rate.

Unpaid collections 25 cents, unless protested, then 50 cents, besides expense of protest.

STOCKS AND BONDS.—Stocks, bonds, promissory notes, unfinished and cancelled bank notes, will be charged at *one half* the regular bank note rate.

LETTERS AND ORDERS.—Letters and orders, unless containing money, or upon the company's business, must not be taken except they are enclosed in a Government Stamped Envelope of the proper denomination, and the same cancelled, (by drawing a pen through the stamp) before forwarding. *Letters enclosed in the ordinary envelope, with postage stamp affixed thereto, will not answer the purpose.* The charge for carrying letters *without value* will be 25 *cents each, prepaid in all cases.* When passing through the hands of other express companies must be charged 25 cents for each company. If value of letters is given and receipted for, the regular money rate must be charged. Orders for goods, to be returned by our company, containing $5.00 or less, will be carried *free,* over that amount will be charged at regular rates.

Corpse.—A corpse of 400 lbs. or under, charged double first class passenger fare over long routes, and three times our freight tariff per 100 lbs. over short routes.

Of Soldiers.—The remains of soldiers of 400 lbs. or less will be charged four cents per mile; excess of that weight at regular rate per 100 lbs. to point of destination, in addition to the four cents per mile. No charge less than $3.00 will be made, and not less than $6.00 when transferred to another express company. The charges on snch business *must, in all cases, be prepaid, or guaranteed by responsible parties.*

Live Stock.—Dogs will be charged at first class passenger fare—must be secured by collar and chain, or in box, *and receipted at owner's risk.* Horses will be charged at double freight rates, estimating each at 2,000 lbs., and *must be receipted at owner's risk,* and in every instance require the *shipper to sign a duplicate receipt to that effect.* No charge less than $25. will be made, however short the distance. Other animals charged in same proportion as for dogs and horses, and must only be taken on same conditions.

No man, woman or child must be taken at any price.

PRODUCE.—Special rates will be given *to dealers* for shipping butter, eggs, game, poultry, fish, oysters, furs, oranges, lemons and fruits, for which application can be made to the Superintendent.

FOREIGN SHIPMENTS.—Goods to and from Canada and other foreign countries must always be accompanied by invoices, and *if destined to the Old Country, prepaid.*

STAMP TAX.—In accordance with Sec. 105 of the Stamp Tax Act, Agents and Messengers will, on and after the 1st day of October, 1862, be provided, at our expense, with stamps, required under said act, and for every article forwarded thereafter will give a receipt, on which shall be affixed and cancelled, a government stamp. If the charge to be collected for the transportation is not to exceed 25 cents—use a stamp of one cent. If the *charge to destination* exceed 25 cents, and is not to exceed one dollar—use a stamp of two cents. If the *charge to destination* on one or more articles, to same address, is to exceed one dollar—use a stamp of five cents.

In cases where it is impracticable to give receipts, a stamp must be affixed to the article sent. This stamp must be of the proper value *according to the rate of charge to be collected to destination*, and *must be cancelled* before leaving your custody.

Your *rule* must be to stamp the receipt, the *exception* can be to stamp the package; if the latter, keep note of the fact in your Way-Bill book, that you may testify to the same in the event of the stamp getting off the package.

Your particular attention is called to the following extracts from the law, its penalties, &c., &c.

EXTRACTS.

Sec. 105. *And be it further enacted,* That on and after the date on which this act shall take effect, no express company or its agent or employee shall receive for transportation from any person any bale, bundle, box, article, or package of any description, without either delivering to the consignor thereof a printed receipt, having stamped or affixed thereon a stamp denoting the duty imposed by this act, or without affixing thereto an adhesive stamp or stamps denoting such duty, and in default thereof shall incur a penalty of ten dollars: *Provided,* That but one stamped receipt or stamp shall be required for each shipment from one party to another party at the same time, whether such shipment consists of one or more packages: *And provided, also,* That no stamped receipts or stamps shall be required for any bale, bundle, box, article or package transported for the government, nor for such bales, bundles, boxes, or packages as are transported by such companies *without charge thereon.*

Sec. 99. *And be it further enacted,* That in any and all cases where an adhesive stamp shall be used for denoting any duty imposed by this act, except as hereinafter provided, the person using or affixing the same shall write thereon the initials of his name, and the date upon which the same shall be attached or used, so that the same may not again be used. And if any person shall fraudulently make use of an adhesive stamp to denote any duty imposed by this act, without so effectually cancelling and obliterating such stamp, except as before mentioned, he, she, or they shall forfeit the sum of fifty dollars.

Express.—For every receipt issued by an express company, or carrier, or person whose occupation it is to act as such, for all boxes, bales, packages, articles, or bundles, for the transportation of which such company, carrier, or person, shall receive a compensation of not over twenty-five cents, one cent.

When such compensation exceeds the sum of twenty-five cents, and not over one dollar, two cents.

When one or more packages are sent to the same address at the same time, and the compensation therefor exceeds one dollar, five cents.

YEARLY OR SEASON CONTRACTS.

A deduction is made from the regular rate on Bank Notes, Stocks and Bonds, where a party will enter into a written guarantee to pay $100 or more, yearly, for such business. Application for contracts must be made to the Superintendent.

CLASSIFICATION OF OFFICES.

Offices printed thus, **Cincinnati,** are common points with the United States Express Company, and are called "Transfer Offices."

Offices printed thus, *Amherst,* are exclusive offices of the United States Express Company.

All other offices are exclusive offices of the American Express Company.

Those marked with a star, (*), are called Non-Reporting Offices.

DIRECTIONS FOR RECEIVING AND MAKING WAY-BILLS TO SAME.

An agent at a common point is allowed to receive and bill all matter offered for other common points, unless acting as an agent for both Companies, in which case he will bill according to joint instructions given him by Superintendents of the two Companies.

No agent at a common point is allowed to receive matter for an exclusive office of the United States Express Company, except by special instructions.

Matter for exclusive points of the United States Express Company must be billed to the "Transfer Office," most direct from point of shipment, and nearest to destination of package.

Matter for Non-Reporting Offices must be billed to office at end of route upon which the same is located and in the direction the article may be going.

INSTRUCTIONS FOR MAKING WAY-BILLS

)F MATTER DESTINED TO PRINCIPAL POINTS IN EASTERN AND NEW ENGLAND DIVISIONS OF AMERICAN EXPRESS COMPANY, AND FOR SAME ON ROUTES OF CONNECTING EXPRESS COMPANIES.

latter destined to the different points named below, must be billed as directed opposite of same, and directly under the name of State in which the office billing is located.

FOR	Offices in NEW YORK, Will bill to	Offices in PENNSYLVANIA, Will bill to	Offices in OHIO, Will bill to	Offices in MICHIGAN, Will bill to	Offices in INDIANA, Will bill to	Offices in KENTUCKY, Will bill to	Offices in ILLINOIS, Will bill to	Offices in WISCONSIN, Will bill to	Offices in MISSOURI, Will bill to	Offices in IOWA, Will bill to	Offices in CANADA WEST, Will bill to
TREAL, C. W.	Buffalo,	Buffalo,	Buffalo,	FREIGHT TO DETROIT, MONEY TO HAMILTON, C. W.	Buffalo, (2)	Buffalo,	FREIGHT TO DETROIT, MONEY TO HAMILTON, C. W.	FREIGHT TO DETROIT, MONEY TO HAMILTON, C. W.	FREIGHT TO DETROIT, MONEY TO HAMILTON, C. W.	FREIGHT TO DETROIT, MONEY TO HAMILTON, C. W.	Hamilton,
BEC, C. E.	“	“	“		“ (2)	“					“
TLAND, Me.	“	“	“	Money and Valuables to Buffalo, Freight to Suspension Bridge.	“	“	Money and Valuables to Buffalo, Freight to Suspension Bridge.	Money and Valuables to Buffalo, Freight to Suspension Bridge.	Money and Valuables to Buffalo, Freight to Suspension Bridge. (3)	Money and Valuables to Buffalo, Freight to Suspension Bridge.	Money and Valuables to Buffalo, Freight to Suspension Bridge. (3)
'ON, Mass.	“	“	“		“	“					
NGFIELD, Mass.	“	“	“		“	“					
VIDENCE, R. I.	“	“	“		“	“					
TFORD, Ct.	“	“	“		“	“					
HAVEN, Ct.	“	“	“		“	“					
ANY, N. Y.	“	“	“		“	“					
YORK CITY.	“	“	“		“	“					
ADELPHIA, Pa.	“	“	“ (1)		“ (1)	“	Chicago, (3)	Chicago,		Chicago,	
RISBURG, “	Cleveland,	Cleveland,	Cleveland (1)	Cleveland,	Crestline,	Crestline,	“ (3)	“	Crestline,	“	
SBURGH, “	“	“	“ (1)	“	“	“	“ (3)	“	“	“	
TIMORE, Md.	Buffalo,	Buffalo,	Buffalo, (1)	MONEY TO BUFFALO, FREIGHT TO SUSPENSION BRIDGE.	Buffalo, (1)	Buffalo,	“ (3)	“	Buffalo,	“	
HINGTON, D. C.	“	“	“ (1)		“ (1)	“	“ (3)	“	“	“	

(1) Except offices located on the line of P. F. W. & C. R. R. They will bill to Crestline, Ohio.
(2) “ “ “ “ “ “ “ Michigan Central and Joliet Cut-off. They will bill freight to Detroit, money and valuables to Hamilton, C. W.
(3) “ “ “ “ “ “ “ T. H. A. & St. L. and the Buff. & L. H. R. R. They will bill to Buffalo.

TARIFF OF RATES

ON PACKAGES OF BANK NOTES IN AMOUNTS UNDER **$600**; AND GOLD AND SILVER IN AMOUNTS UNDER **$500.**

Where Rates on Bank Notes are ☞	**50 Cents Per $1,000.**			**75 Cents Per $1,000.**			**$1.00 Per $1,000.**			**$1.25 & $1.50 Per $1,000.**			**$1.75 & $2.00 Per $1,000.**			**$2.25 & $2.50 Per $1,000.**			**$2.75 & $3.00 Per $1,000.**			**$3.25 & $3.50 Per $1,000.**			**$3.75 & $4.00 Per $1,000.**			**$4.25 t Per $**	
CHARGE ON PACKAGES OF	NOTES.	GOLD.	SILVER	NOTES.	GOLD.	SILVER	NOTES.	GOLD.	SILVER	NOTES.	GOLD.	SILVER	NOTES.	GOLD.	SILVER	NOTES.	GOLD.	SILVER	NOTES.	GOLD.	SILVER	NOTES.	GOLD.	SILVER	NOTES.	GOLD.	SILVER	NOTES.	
$25 or less......	25	25	25	30	30	30	30	30	50	50	60	70	75	75	80	75	1.00	1.00	1.00	1.25	1.25	1.00	1.25	1.50	1.00	1.25	1.50	1.25	1.
Over 25 to $50......	25	25	40	30	30	50	30	40	60	60	70	80	75	80	1.00	80	1.00	1.20	1.00	1.25	1.50	1.00	1.25	1.75	1.00	1.25	1.75	1.25	1.
" 50 " 75......	30	30	40	30	30	60	40	40	70	70	75	1.00	80	1.00	1.25	1.00	1.25	1.50	1.00	1.25	1.75	1.25	1.50	2.25	1.25	1.50	2.25	1.50	1.
" 75 " 100......	30	30	50	30	30	70	50	50	80	80	90	1.25	1.00	1.00	1.75	1.00	1.25	2.25	1.25	1.75	2.50	1.50	2.00	2.75	1.50	2.00	3.00	1.75	2.
" 100 " 200......	30	40	50	40	50	80	50	60	1.00	90	1.00	1.50	1.00	1.25	2.50	1.25	1.50	3.00	1.50	2.00	3.25	1.75	2.25	3.50	1.75	2.25	4.00	2.00	2.
" 200 " 300......	35	50	60	50	60	1.00	60	70	1.25	1.00	1.25	2.00	1.25	1.25	3.00	1.50	1.75	3.75	2.00	2.25	4.00	2.25	2.50	5.00	2.25	2.50	5.00	2.50	2
" 300 " 400......	40	50	75	60	70	1.25	70	80	1.50	1.00	1.25	2.50	1.25	1.50	3.50	1.75	2.00	4.50	2.25	2.50	5.00	2.50	2.75	6.00	2.50	2.75	6.00	2.75	3.
" 400 " 500	40	60	90	70	75	1.50	80	1.00	2.00	1.25	1.50	3.00	1.50	1.75	4.00	2.00	2.25	5.00	2.50	2.75	6.00	2.75	3.25	7.00	3.00	3.25	7.00	3.50	3
" 500 " 600......	50	60	....	75	90	....	90	1.30	....	1.25	1.50	....	1.75	2.00	....	2.25	2.50	....	2.75	3.00	....	3.25	3.75	....	3.50	4.00	....	4.25	4.

Explanation of Tariff.—For instance, you wish to make a rate on package of notes, gold or silver, of from $200 to $300 to a point where the rate per $1,00 on notes is $1.50; refer to amount of package on left hand column, "$200 to $300," trace the line to column "$1.25 to $1.50" per $1,000, and it gives the charg on notes, $1.00; gold, $1.25; and silver, $2.00.

Packages of bank notes of $600 and under $1,000, charge same as $1,000; over $1,000, at the rate per thousand on actual amount of package.

Packages of gold and silver of $500 and upwards, destined to points where the tariff on same is $2.00 or more per $1,000, will be charged at regular tariff pe thousand for actual amount of package.

TARIFF OF RATES

ON BOXES AND PACKAGES OF ORDINARY VALUE AND BULK WEIGHING *LESS* THAN **50** POUNDS.

WHERE RATE **On Freight is** ☞	50 cts per 100 lbs.	75 cts per 100 lbs.	$1.00 per 100 lbs.	$1.25 per 100 lbs.	$1.50 per 100 lbs.	$1.75 & $2.00 per 100 lbs.	$2.25 & $2.50 per 100 lbs.	$2.75 & $3.00 per 100 lbs.	$3.25 to $4.00 per 100 lbs.	$4.25 to $5.00 per 100 lbs.	$5.25 to $6.00 per 100 lbs.	$6.25 to $7 00 per 100 lbs.	$7.25 to $8.00 per 100 lbs.	$8.25 to $9.00 per 100 lbs.	$9 10 1
Charges on Single Pack'gs not Exceeding Six Inches Square,	25	25	30	35	40	50	60	75	75	1.00	1.25	1.50	1.75	2.00	
Packages of 10 lbs or under..	25	25	30	40	50	60	75	90	1.00	1.25	1.50	1.75	2.00	2.25	
10 to 20 lbs..............	25	30	40	50	60	75	90	1.00	1.25	1.50	1.75	2.00	2.25	2.50	
20 to 30 lbs..............	30	40	50	60	75	90	1.00	1.25	1.40	1.75	2.00	2.25	2.50	3.00	
30 to 40 lbs..............	35	50	60	70	80	1.00	1.25	1.40	1.50	2.00	2.25	2.50	3.00	3.50	
40 to 50 lbs..............	40	60	70	80	90	1.25	1.50	1.75	2.00	2.50	3.00	3.50	4.00	4.50	

Boxes or packages of 50 lbs. and upwards, charge regular tariff per 100 pounds. Packages of books, stationery, news papers or magazines, *to dealers*, weighing 30 lbs. and upwards, charge regular tariff rate per 100 for *actual* weight; under 30 pounds, charge per table of rates given above. *Packages which must pass through the hands of other Express Companies, before reaching destination, will be charged one-half more than the rate given above, to all points where the through rate per hundred lbs. is* $1.50 *or less, and never less than* 25 *cts. per package for each company.* Extra bulky packages will be charged one-half more than ordinary tariff rate. Packages valued at over $50 will be charged 25 cts. extra for each $100 in value, which value must always be marked on outside of package, and entered upon Way Bill. Agents *may, at their discretion*, carry the smallest class of packages, such as daguerreotypes, &c., at less than the above rates, to points where the tariff per 100 pounds is $2.50, or more.

For explantion of above tariff, see tariff on packages, bank notes, gold and silver, under $600.

American Express Company.

Through Rates to Principal points in Eastern and New England Divisions of American Express Company, and those on Routes of Connecting Express Companies.

FROM Como Ill TO	Bank Notes per $1,000. $600 Equal to $1000.	Freight per 100 lbs. for 50 lbs. and upwards.	Special Rates or Remarks.
ALBANY, ... N. Y.	2 00	4 25	4 75
NEW YORK, ... "	2 00	4 25	5.50
BOSTON, ... MASS.	2 50	4 75	6.00
SPRINGFIELD, ... "	"	"	"
HARTFORD, ... Ct.	2 75	5 00	"
NEW HAVEN, ... "	"	"	"
PROVIDENCE, ... R. I.	"	"	"
PHILADELPHIA, ... Pa.	2 00	4 25	5 25
PITTSBURG, ... "	"	3 00	3 75
HARRISBURG, ... "	3 25	4 25	4 50
BALTIMORE, ... Md.	2 00	4 25	5 25
WASHINGTON, ... D. C.	2 50	5 75	5 50
PORTLAND, ... Me.	3 75	7 00	8.00
QUEBEC, ... C. E.	3 50	6 50	7 50
MONTREAL, ... "	3 00	5 00	6.00

FROM Como Ill TO	Bank Notes per $1000. $600 Equal to $1000.	Freight per 100 lbs for 50 lbs and upwards.	Sepccial Rates or Remerks.

FROM Como Ill TO	Bank Notes per $1000. — $600 Equal to $1000.	Freight per 100 lbs for 50 lbs and upwards.	Special rates or Remarks.
*ANGOLA, ... N. Y.	175	300	450
BUFFALO, (local tariff) "	175	300	"
" (thro' ") "	150	275	400
DUNKIRK, (" ") "	175	300	"
" (local ") "	"	"	480
*IRVING, ... "	"	"	"
JAMESTOWN, ... "	200	350	480
*MAYVILLE, ... "	"	"	"
*QUINCY, ... "	175	300	400
SUSPENSION BRIDGE, (local tariff,) "	"	"	"
SUSPENSION BRIDGE, (thro' tariff) "	175	300	350
SILVER CREEK, ... "	175	300	400
WESTFIELD, ... "	175	300	400
State Line			"
North Evans			480
Brockton			4.
Portland			"
Mayville			600

FROM Como Ill TO	Bank Notes per $1000 / $600 Equal to $1000.	Freight per 100 lbs for 50 lbs and upwards.	Special Rates or Remarks.
ACTON, ... C. W.	200	300	375
*BADEN, ... "	200	300	"
BEAMSVILLE, ... "	175	250	350
BEACHVILLE, ... "	"	"	"
BERLIN, ... "	200	300	375
BOUTHWELL, ... "	175	250	350
BRAMPTON, ... "	200	300	375
BRANTFORD, ... "	175	300	"
CALEDONIA, ... "	175	300	"
CHATHAM, ... "	175	300	350
CLIFTON, ... "	175	300	"
CLINTON, ... "	225	350	425
*CARRON BROOK, ... "	225	325	4.00
*CRAIGS, ... "	200	275	350
DUNDAS, ... "	175	300	350
DUNNVILLE, ... "	175	300	375
FORT ERIE, ... "	175	300	350
GALT, ... "	175	300	375
GEORGETOWN, ... "	200	300	"
GOODERICH, ... "	225	350	350
GLENCOE, ... "	225	325	375
GRIMSBY, ... "	175	250	425
GUELPH, ... "	200	300	"
HAMILTON, ... "	175	300	350
HAMBURGH, ... "	175	250	"
*HARPEN HAY, ... "	225	350	"
KOMOCA, ... "	175	250	375
LONDON, ... "	175	300	425
*LUCAN, ... "	200	275	350

FROM *Como Que* TO	Bank Notes per $1000. $600 Equal to $1000.	Freight per 100 lbs for 50 lbs and upwards.	Special Rates, or Remarks.
MALTON, ... C. W.	2 00	3 00	4 25
MITCHELL, ... "	2 25	3 25	3 50
MT BRYDGES, ... "	"	"	3 75
NEWBURY, ... "	"	"	"
ONTARIO, ... "	"	"	4
PARIS, ... "	1 75	3 00	4
PETERSBURGH, ... "	2 00	3 00	"
PLATTSVILLE, ... "			"
PORT COLBORNE, ... "	1 75	3 00	3 50
PORT STANLEY, ... "	1 75	3 00	"
PRESTON, ... "	1 75	2 50	3 75
PRINCETON, ... "	"	"	3 50
*ROCKWOOD, ... "	2 00	3 00	3 75
SARNIA, ... "	"	"	3 50
ST. CATHARINES, ... "	1 75	3 00	3 75
ST. MARYS, ... "	2 00	2 75	4
ST. THOMAS, ... "	1 75	3 00	3 50
STRATFORD, ... "	2 00	3 00	4
STRATHROY, ... "	"	"	3 50
SEAFORTH, ... "	2 25	3 50	3 75
*SHAKSPEARE, ... "	2 00	3 00	"
THAMESVILLE, ... "	1 75	2 50	3 50
THOROLD, ... "	"	"	4
TORONTO, ... "	2 00	3 00	4 25
*WIDDER, ... "	"	2 75	3 50
*WINDSOR, ... "	1 75	2 25	3 75
WOODSTOCK, ... "	1 75	3 00	3 50
*WESTON, ... "	2 00	3 00	[illegible]
*WYOMING, ... "	"	"	

FROM Como Ill TO	Bank Notes per $1000 — $600 Equal to $1000.	Freight per 100 lbs for 50 lbs and upwards.	Special Rates or Remarks.
x Tlespaler	150	350	

FROM Como Ill TO	Bank Notes per $1000. $600 Equal to $1000.	Freight per 100 lbs for 50 lbs and upwards.	Special rates or Remarks. Cy } Sct	
*ALBION, ... Penn.	200	300	375	
*COLUMBUS, ... "	225	325	500	
CONNEAUTVILLE, ... "	200	300	350	Sha
*CONCORD, ... "	"	325	475	
CORRY, ... "	"	"	"	
ERIE, ... "	~~175~~	275	200 } 450	
*ESPYVILLE, ... "	225	325	600	
*FAIRVIEW, ... "	175	250	400	
FRANKLIN, ... "	225	375	Closed	
GIRARD, ... "	150	275	400	
IRVINE, ... "	175	300	600	
*JAMESTOWN, ... "	225	325	"	
*LINESVILLE, ... "	"	"	"	
MEADVILLE, ... "	175	325	500	Closed
*McLEANS, ... "	225	325	600	
NORTH EAST .... "	175	325	425	
*PITTSFIELD, ... "	225	325	525	
SPRINGFIELD, ... "	150	275	400	
TITUSVILLE, ... "	250	400	600	
UNION MILLS, ... "	200	300	500	
WATERFORD, ... "	"	"	"	
WARREN, ... "	225	325	525	
WEST GREENVILLE, . "	"	"	570	
*YOUNGSVILLE, ... "	"	"	525	
[illegible]			525	Closed
*Centreville	250	400	650	Shaffer
*Spartansburg	"	"	650	
Shamrock			625	
Frizonville			650	Shaffer

o Rec'pt and Bill to Erie

FROM Como Ill TO	Bank Notes per $1000. / $600 Equal to $1000.	Freight per 100 lbs for 50 lbs and upwards.	Special Rates or Remarks.
Wilcox			2.25 5.75
Winne			" "
Sheffield			" "
Shaffer			2.50 6.75
Ridgway			2.25 5.75
[illegible]			" [illegible]

FROM Como Ill TO		Bank Notes per $1,000. $600 Equal to $1000.	Freight per 100 lbs. for 50 lbs. and upwards.	Special Rates or Remarks.
*_Amherst,_	Ohio,	150	275	400
ASHTABULA,........	"	150	275	"
*ASHLEY,...........	"	150	275	375
*_Antwerp,_	"	125	250	450
*_Arcanum,_	"	150	225	475
*_Archibald,_	"	125	200	275
X **Berea,**............	"	150	275	375
*_Berlin,_	"	150	275	375
Bellevue,...........	"	150	275	400
BUCYRUS, ...	"	150	275	325
Bryan, ...	"	150	200	275
Bellefontaine, ...	"	150	275	450
Belleville, ...	"	150	250	400
Belle Centre, ...	"	150	200	"
CARDINGTON, ...	"	150	275	375
CAMDEN, ...	"	150	275	"
Carey, ...	"	150	275	4,
Carlisle, ...	"	150	275	475
* _Caledonia,_.........	"	150	300	450
CEDARVILLE,........	"	150	275	400
Cincinnati, ...	"	150	375	Dst 375
Cleveland, ...	"	150	275	350
Clyde,.............	"	150	275	4.00
CONNEAUT, ...	"	150	275	"
u S – COLLEGE CORNERS,.	"	150	250	475
Columbus,........	"	150	275	425
Columbus Grove,...	"	150	250	450
CORWIN, ...	"	150	250	400
Covington, ...	"	"	"	450

FROM Como Ill TO	Bank Notes per $1000. $600 Equal to $1000.	Freight per 100 lbs for 50 lbs and upwards.	Special Rates or Remarks.
Crestline, ... Ohio.	150	275	[illegible]
* *Castalia,* .... "	"	225	375
* *Carthage,* .... "	"	250	"
* *Cumminsville,* ...... "	"	"	"
* *Criderville,* .... "	"	225	475
CAMP DENNISON .... "	175	200	4.
*COLLINSVILLE, ... "	150	250	375
Dayton, ... "	150	275	"
* *De Graff,* .... "	150	300	450
Defiance, ... "	125	250	"
DELPHOS, ... "	150	275	375
Delaware, ... "	150	275	375
* *Delta,* .... "	"	200	400
* *Dallas,* .... "	"	225	475
EATON, ... "	150	300	375
* *Elmore,* .... "	150	275	"
Elyria, ... "	150	275	4.
Edgerton, ... "	150	225	275
*EUCLID, ... "	150	250	375
*ELDORADO, ... "	150	275	350
Findlay, ... "	150	225	4.00
Forest, ... "	150	275	325
Fostoria, ... "	150	225	4.
Fremont, ... "	150	275	"
Fredericktown, ... "	150	275	450
*FORT ANCIENT, ... "	150	250	4.
*FLORENCE, ... "	"	275	375
*FOSTER'S CROSSINGS, "	"	250	4.
Galion, ... "	150	275	375

FROM Como Ill TO	Bank Notes; per $1000. / $600 Equal to $1000.	Freight per 100 lbs for 50 lbs and upwards.	Special rates or Remarks.
GREENWICH, ...Ohio.	150	275	375
GENEVA, ... "	150	275	4.
GILEAD, ... "	150	275	375
Grafton, ... "	150	275	"
Greenville, ... "	150	275	475
Glendale, ... "	150	225	375
Hamilton, ... "	150	275	"
**Havana*, ... "	150	275	4.
Huron, ... "	150	275	
**Huntsville*, ... "	150	275	400
*IBERIA, ... "	150	275	375
**Independence*, ... "	150	250	"
*JOHNSTOWN, ... "	150	225	3.
Kenton, ... "	150	275	4.
KINGSVILLE, ... "	150	275	"
*KIRKERSVILLE, ... "	150	250	450
LEBANON, ... "	175	300	400
Lima, ... "	150	275	3.
London, ... "	150	275	400
**La Rue*, ... "	"	"	400
**Leipsic*, ... "	150	250	4.
**Ludlow*, ... "	"	"	375
**Lexington*, ... "	"	"	400
**Lockland*, ... "	"	"	375
*LAGRANGE, ... "	150	225	"
*LOVELAND, ... "	175	300	4.
*LEWIS CENTRE, ... "	150	250	"
*LAFAYETTE, ... "	"	"	375
MADISON, ... "	150	275	375

FROM Como Ill TO	Bank Notes per $1000 — $600 Equal to $1000.	Freight per 100 lbs for 50 lbs and upwards.	Special Rates or Remarks.
Mansfield, ... Ohio.	150	275	450
Marion, ... "	150	300	"
Marysville, ... "	150	275	4.
Maumee City, ... "	125	225	325
Mechanicsburg, ... "	"	"	4.
Miamisburgh, ... "	150	275	475
Middletown, ... "	150	275	"
*MILFORD,... "	175	300	4.
Monroeville, ... "	150	275	275
MORROW, ... "	150	275	4.
Mt. Vernon, ... "	150	275	450
Mt. Victory, ... "	150	175	"
*MANCHESTER,....... "	150	225	350
Napoleon, ... "	125	225	325
Newark, ... "	150	275	450
NEW LONDON,...... "	150	275	375
NEW PARIS,........ "	150	300	4.50
Norwalk, ... "	125	275	4.
**New Westfield,* ..... "	150	275	450
*NEVADA,.......... "	150	250	325
Oberlin, ... "	150	275	4.
**Olmsted Falls,* ...... "	150	275	375
**Osborne,* .... "	150	275	"
**Ottawa,* .... "	150	250	4.
OXFORD, ... "	"	"	475
**Ostrander,* .... "	"	"	4.
PAINESVILLE,....... "	150	275	375
Perrysburgh, ... "	150	250	400
Piqua, ... "	150	275	475

FROM Como Ill TO	Bank Notes per $1000. — $600 Equal to $1000.	Freight per 100 lbs for 50 lbs and upwards.	Special Rates, or Remarks.
Plymouth, ... Ohio.	150	275	450
* *Post Town,* .... "	150	250	375
* *Pleasant Valley,* .... "	150	225	475
*Pataskala,.......... "	150	250	450
* *Quincy,* .... "	150	275	"
* *Ridgeway,* .... "	150	175	"
* *Rushsylvania,* ...... "	"	"	"
*ROCHESTER, ... "	150	250	375
Sandusky, ... "	150	300	"
*SAYBROOK, ... "	150	275	4.
Shelby, ... "	150	275	375
Sidney, ... "	150	275	475
SONORO, ... "	150	225	450
S. CHARLESTON, ... "	150	300	"
Springfield, ... "	150	275	"
Stryker, ... "	150	225	275
* *Sylvania,* .... "	150	275	"
*SALEM, .. Shiloh "	150	250	375
*SPRING VALLEY, ... "	"	"	4.
*SELMA, ... "	"	"	"
*SEVEN MILES, ... "	"	"	375
*SOMERVILLE, ... "	"	275	"
* *St. Paris,* .... "	"	220	475
Tiffin, ... "	150	200	4.
Tippecanoe, ... "	150	275	475
Toledo, ... "	150	275	275
* *Townsend,* .... "	150	200	375
Troy, ... "	150	275	475
* *Trenton,* .... "	"	250	375

FROM Como Ill. TO	Bank Notes per $1000. — $600 Equal to $1000.	Freight per 100 lbs for 50 lbs and upwards.	Special rates or Remarks.
* *Tonogany,* .... Ohio.	[illegible]	[illegible]	4.
Union City,... Ohio & Ind.	150	300	475
*Unionville, ... Ohio.	150	275	375
Upper Sandusky,... "	150	275	325
Urbana, ... "	150	275	475
* *Utica,* .... "	150	275	375
Van Wert,........ "	150	275	275
* *Vermillion,* .... "	150	275	4.
* *Versailles,* .... "	150	300	475
Wakeman,......... "	150	275	4.
Wauseon,......... "	150	[illegible]	275
Wapakoneta, ... "	"	"	475
Wellington, ... "	150	275	375
*West Jefferson,... "	150	275	425
West Liberty,...... "	150	275	475
* *White Sulph. Sp'gs,* "	150	[illegible]	4
Willoughby, ... "	150	275	375
Worthington,..... "	150	[illegible]	4.
* *Washington,* .... "	150	225	"
* *Woodstock,*......... "	"	[illegible]	375
* *West Cairo,*........ "	"	"	4.
Xenia, ... "	150	275	"
Yellow Springs,... "	150	275	"
Zanesville,....... "	150	275	475
West Manchester	125	350	
Dodson Sta	"	"	
Brookville	"	"	
[illegible]	125	350	
[illegible]	"	400	

FROM Como Ill TO	Bank Notes per $1000 / $600 Equal to $1000.	Freight per 100 lbs for 50 lbs and upwards.	Special Rates or Remarks.
Dover	125	400	
Marston	"	575	
Perry	"	"	
Milford Center	"	425	
Davis	"	4.	
Clay Coals	"	475	
[illegible]	100	325	
Blackwick	125	450	
Shiloh (Galena)	"	375	
Ward (M Center)	"	425	
Freeport	"	4.	

FROM Como Ill TO		Bank Notes per $1000. / $600 Equal to $1000.	Freight per 100 lbs for 50 lbs and upwards.	Special rates or Remarks.
ANDERSON, ...	Ind.	150	200	300
Attica, ...	"	125	225	400
*ARCADIA, ...	"	150	275	350
BAINBRIDGE,........	"	"	225	475
BRADFORD,.........	"	100	200	325
BRAZIL, ...	"	125	250	350
Bristol,............	"	125	200	250
*[illegible],........	"	150	275	[illegible]
*BATTLE GROUND, ...	"	125	250	325
BROOKSTON,........	"	"	"	"
**Butler*,.............	"	"	"	275
*BLOOM,.............	"			8
*BUENA VISTA.......	"	150	275	325
*BELLEVILLE, ...	"	125	250	375
*BROWNSVILLE, ...	"	175	325	475
*BOURBON,..........	"	125	175	200
CAMBRIDGE CITY,...	"	150	300	375
**Calumet*, ...	"	125	175	2.
CENTERVILLE, ...	"	150	300	375
**Chesterfield*,........	"	150	300	325
CICERO, ...	"	150	275	350
COLUMBIA CITY, ...	"	150	250	250
CONNERSVILLE,.....	"	175	325	500
CRAWFORDSVILLE,...	"	150	275	450
**Carpenters*, ...	"	125	250	375
*CHARLOTTSVILLE,....	"	150	275	400
*CLEVELAND, ...	"	"	"	"
*COFFIN'S STATION,..	"	125	200	"
*CUMBERLAND, ...	"	150	275	"

FROM Como Ill. TO	Bank Notes per $1,000. $600 Equal to $1000.	Freight per 100 lbs. for 50 lbs. and upwards.	Special Rates or Remarks.
*COLFAX, ... Ind.	[illegible]	[illegible]	375
*CLARK'S HILL, ... "	"	"	"
*CASSVILLE, ... "	[illegible]	[illegible]	275
*CASTLETON, ... "	[illegible]	290	350
*CARTERSBURGH, ... "	"	"	375
*COATSVILLE, ... "	"	"	"
*CRITTENDEN, ... "	1[illegible]	[illegible]	"
*CARPENTERSVILLE, .. "	100	27[illegible]	475
*CORWIN, ... "	"	225	4
Delphi, ... "	150	250	"
DUBLIN, ... "	1[illegible]	200	"
*DYER, ... "	100	100	175
Elkhart, ... "	125	200	225
*ETNA GREEN, ... "	12[illegible]	170	200
Fort Wayne, ... "	125	250	250
*FRANCESVILLE, ... "	100	[illegible]	275
**Farmland*, ... "	100	275	475
**Fortville*, ... "	12[illegible]	280	375
*FRANKTON, ... "	1[illegible]	225	275
*FAIRFIELD, ... "	100	250	4
*FILLMORE, ... "	100	270	"
Goshen, ... "	125	200	3
GREENFIELD, ... "	150	300	4
GREENCASTLE, ... "	125	275	475
*GIBSON, ... "	70	120	175
*GALVESTON, ... "	100	[illegible]	275
*GERMANTOWN, ... "	"	"	4
HAGERSTOWN, ... "	150	300	325
Huntington, ... "	125	250	3[illegible]

FROM Como Ill TO		Bank Notes per \$1000. \$600 Equal to \$1000.	Freight per 100 lbs for 50 lbs and upwards.	Special Rates or Remarks.
*HIGHLAND, ...	Ind.	125	250	375
*HUNTSVILLE, ...	"	150	280	250
*HANNAH, ...	"	125	175	175
*HOBART, ...	"	75	125	150
Indianapolis, ...	"	125	275	375
Kendalville, ...	"	125	200	250
KNIGHTSTOWN,......	"	150	300	375
KOKOMO, ...	"	150	300	275
**Kent*,..............	"	100	150	175
LADOGA, ...	"	150	275	475
Lafayette, ...	"	100	200	325
Lagro, ...	"	125	250	375
Laporte,..........	"	125	175	175
LAKE STATION, ...	"	125	150	150
LEBANON,..........	"	150	275	375
LEWISVILLE, ...	"	150	200	4.
LIBERTY, ...	"	150	200	475
Ligonier, ...	"	150	200	275
Logansport,......	"	125	250	250
*LINCOLN,..........	"	150	275	275
MICHIGAN CITY,....	"	125	150	225
MIDDLETOWN, ...	"	150	300	275
**Middlebury*,........	"	125	200	250
Mishawaka,........	"	125	200	"
Monticello, ...	"	"	"	4.
Muncie,............	"	150	300	475
**Marshfield*,........	"	150	200	250
**Morristown*, ...	"	150	275	525
*MILLVILLE,.........	"	"	"	2.

FROM Cairo Ill TO		Bank Notes per $1000 — $600 Equal to 1000.	Freight per 100 lbs for 50 lbs and upwards.	Special Rates or Remarks.
*MEDARYVILLE, ...	Ind.	[illegible]	[illegible]	325
*MIAMI, ...	"	[illegible]	[illegible]	3.
**New Carlisle*, ...	"	125	175	175
NEW CASTLE, ...	"	150	300	3.
NOBLESVILLE, ...	"	150	300	375
*NEVADA, ...	"	[illegible]	[illegible]	275
**Oakland*, ...	"	[illegible]	[illegible]	375
*OGDEN, ...	"	[illegible]	[illegible]	4
**Pendleton*, ...	"	[illegible]	[illegible]	325
Peru, ...	"	100	250	3.
Plymouth, ...	"	125	175	175
*PHILADELPHIA, ...	"	[illegible]	[illegible]	4
*PLAINFIELD, ...	"		[illegible]	"
*PORTER'S STATION, ..	"	[illegible]	[illegible]	150
QUINCY, ...	"	[illegible]	[illegible]	250
REYNOLDS, ...	"	100	[illegible]	375
RICHMOND, ...	"	150	300	325
ROCKVILLE, ...	"	[illegible]	[illegible]	"
**Rolling Prairie*, ...	"	[illegible]	[illegible]	[illegible]
**Rome*, ...	"	[illegible]	[illegible]	175
*ROYAL CENTRE, ...	"	"	"	[illegible]
*RAYSVILLE, ...	"	[illegible]	[illegible]	250
*REELSVILLE, ...	"	[illegible]	[illegible]	4.
*ROSEDALE, ...	"	"	"	375
*ROSS, ...	"	[illegible]	100	"
**Smithfield*, ...	"	150	300	175
South Bend, ...	"	125	175	475
**Sheldon*, ...	"			350
*SULPHUR SPRINGS, ...	"	[illegible]	[illegible]	3

FROM Como Ill. TO	Bank Notes per $1000. $600 Equal to $1000.	Freight per 100 lbs for 50 lbs and upwards.	Special Rates or Remarks.
State Line,......... Ind.	100	100	4
*STOCKWELL,....... “	100	200	375
*SAN PIERRE, ... “	100	200	275
*SHARPSVILLE,....... “	100	275	3
*STAUNTON, ... “	125	250	375
*ST. MARY'S, ... “	125	225	325
TERRE HAUTE, ... “	125	250	350
THORNTOWN, ... “	150	275	375
TIPTON,............ “	150	300	325
VALPARAISO, ... “	75	120	175
Wabash, ... “	125	250	375
WARSAW, ... “	150	225	2
Waterloo, ... “	150	250	325
WESTVILLE, ... “	150	225	250
Williamsport, ... “	100	200	4
Winchester, ... “	150	300	475
WINAMAC, ... “	100	250	225
*WASHINGTON,....... “	150	275	325
*WINDFALL, ... “	150	225	375
*WHITESTOWN, ... “	"	"	375
*WANATAH, ... “	125	175	2
*WALTON, ... “	150	275	275
* *Yorktown,* .... “	150	300	475
ZIONSVILLE, ... “	150	275	375
* [illegible]	150	200	
Culvers Station "	100	200	325
Bennetts Switch	125	200	
Tammany	100	325	
Florida	125	275	

FROM Como Ill. TO	Bank Notes per $1000 — $600 Equal to $1000.	Freight per 100 lbs for 50 lbs and upwards.	Special Rates or Remarks.
Chatham	100	325	
Clarks Station	100	175	Closed
Ashby Mills	100	475	
Crown Point	100	200	
Catlin	100	375	
Hebron	100	2.	
Augusta	125	375	
Ellaytown	0	4.	
La Clair	100	250	
Scarboro (Colo City)	125	225	
Crease	"	250	
Ashland	100	3	
New Britton	"	375	
North Judson	125	225	

FROM Como Ill TO	Bank Notes per $1000. / $600 Equal to $1000.	Freight per 100 lbs for 50 lbs and upwards.	Special rates or Remarks.	
			[illegible]	[illegible]
LOUISVILLE, ... Ky.	~~150~~	~~300~~	175	425

FROM Como Ill. TO		Bank Notes per $1000. — $600 Equal to $1000.	Freight per 100 lbs for 50 lbs and upwards.	Special Rates, or Remarks.
Adrian,	Mich.	150	200	2 75
ALBION,	"	125	200	"
ANN ARBOR,	"	125	250	3 00
*AUGUSTA,	"	100	[illegible]	2 50
*ADA,	"	[illegible]	[illegible]	4.
BATTLE CREEK,	"	125	200	2 75
**Blissfield*,	"	[illegible]	[illegible]	"
**Bronson*,	"	125	200	"
Burr Oak,	"	125	200	"
*BUCHANAN,	"	[illegible]	[illegible]	2 25
*BEEBEE'S CORNERS,	"	[illegible]	[illegible]	3 25
*BIRMINGHAM,	"	[illegible]	[illegible]	"
*BERLIN,	"	100	[illegible]	4.
CHELSEA,	"	125	250	3.
**Clayton*,	"	150	200	2 75
Clinton,	"	150	200	"
Coldwater,	"	125	200	"
Constantine,	"	[illegible]	[illegible]	"
*CORUNNA,	"	[illegible]	[illegible]	3 75
*CLARKSTON,	"	100	[illegible]	"
*COOPERSVILLE,	"	75	120	4.
*CHAMBERLAINS,	"	[illegible]	200	2 25
Detroit,	"	125	200	3.
DEXTER,	"	125	250	"
DECATUR,	"	125	150	2 10
DOWAGIAC,	"	125	150	"
*DAVISBURG,	"	[illegible]	200	3 75
*DAYTON PLAINS,	"	"	"	3 25
*DAYTON,	"	[illegible]	120	2 25

Dearborn 125 3,00

FROM Como Ill TO	Bank Notes per $1000. / $600 Equal to $1000.	Freight per 100 lbs for 50 lbs and upwards.	Special rates or Remarks.
FENTONVILLE, ... Mich.	125	225	375
*FERRYSBURG, ... "	100	225	4.
GALESBURGH, ... "	125	175	250
GRASS LAKE, ... "	125	250	3.
GRAND HAVEN, ... "	100	225	4.
GRAND RAPIDS, ... "	125	250	〃
*GAINES, ... "	125	225	375
Hillsdale, ... "	150	200	275
Hudson, ... "	150	200	〃
*HOLLEY, ... "	125	225	375
IONIA, ... "	175	275	4.
Jackson, ... "	100	250	275
Jonesville, ... "	150	250	275
KALAMAZOO, ... "	125	175	250
LANSING, ... "	100	225	4
LAWTON, ... "	100	100	250
*LINDEN, ... "	125	200	375
*LEONI, ... "	125	225	3.
*LYONS, ... "	175	275	See Mi
*LANSINGBURG, ... "	150	225	4
*LOWELL, ... "	175	250	〃
Manchester, ... "	150	200	275
MARSHALL, ... "	125	200	〃
MATTAWAN, ... "	125	175	250
Monroe, ... "	150	200	275
*MT. CLEMENS, ... "	150	175	325
*MILL POINT, ... "	100	225	4.
Napoleon, ... "	150	200	275
*NEW BUFFALO, ... "	125	150	225

FROM Como Ill TO	Bank Notes per $1,000. $600 Equal to $1000.	Freight per 100 lbs. for 50 lbs. and upwards.	Special Rates or Remarks.
NILES, ... Mich.	125	150	250
*NEW BALTIMORE,.... "	125	170	325
*NUNNICA, ... "	100	250	4.
OWASSO, ... "	125	250	375
*OVID,.............. "	125	250	″
PARMA, ... "	125	200	275
**Pittsford*, ... "	150	200	275
PONTIAC,........... "	125	225	325
PORT HURON, ... "	150	225	″
*PEWAMO, ... "	175	275	4.
* *Quincy*, ... "	150	200	275
*ROYAL OAK, ... "	125	170	325
*RIDGEWAY,......... "	150	225	″
Sturgis,............ "	125	200	250
ST. JOHNS, ... "	125	250	375
*SARANAC, ... "	150	275	4.
*SMITH'S CREEK,..... "	150	225	325
Tecumseh,.......... "	150	200	275
Three Rivers, ... "	″	″	″
* *Trenton*, ... "	150	200	″
*UTICA ROAD, ... "	125	170	325
*VERNON,........... "	″	225	375
White Pigeon, ... "	125	200	250
*WAYNE, ... "	125	170	3.00
YPSILANTI, ... "	125	250	300
Flint ″	150	275	4.25
East Saginaw ″	175	300	475
x Pine River			250 ″
x Pokagon			125 250

FROM Como Ill TO	Bank Notes per $1000. $600 Equal to $1000.	Freight per 100 lbs for 50 lbs and upwards.	Special Rates or Remarks.
Saginaw City	2 50	5	
Wenona or Lyons	1 75	4	
Bath	2 25	4	
Escanaba	2 50	4 50	
Marquette	2 75	4 75	
Houghton	3 25	5 25	
Hancock	„	„	
Eagle Harbor	„	„	
Copper Harbor	„	„	
Eagle River	„	„	
Ontonagon	„	„	
Sault Ste Marie	2 50	5	
Mt Morris	2 25	4 25	Ex Saginaw
Negaunee	2 75	4 75	

FROM Como Ill. TO		Bank Notes per $1000 — $600 Equal to $1000.	Freight per 100 lbs for 50 lbs and upwards.	Special Rates or Remarks.
Alton, ...	ILL.	150	225	325
AMBOY, ...	"	75	75	275
Annawan, ...	"	125	150	325
Atlanta, ...	"	125	150	275
**Auburn,*	"	150	225	325
AURORA, ...	"	50	100	175
**Athens,*	"	100	100	"
**Atkinson,*	"	100	150	325
ASHMORE, ...	"	"	"	"
*ARLINGTON, ...	"	70	100	275
*AVON,, ...	"	80	100	350
*ABINGDON, ...	"	"	"	325
*ASHKUM, ...	"	100	100	2.
*APPLE RIVER,.......	"	80	120	200
*ASSUMPTION, ...	"	100	100	325
*ALTONA, ...	"	50	100	"
*ALGONQUIN, ...	"	75	100	150
*AUGUSTA, ...	"	100	120	375
BATAVIA, ...	"	50	100	125
Beardstown, ...	"	125	200	4.
BELVIDERE,.........	"	50	125	200
BEMENT,...........	"	150	200	250
**Blue Island,*	"	125	175	200
Bloomington,.....	"	100	150	200
**Bremen,*	"	125	175	200
Brighton, ...	"	150	225	325
BUNKER HILL, ...	"	100	150	"
Bureau Junction,...	"	125	150	200
BUTLER, ...	"	100	120	325

FROM Como Ill TO		Bank Notes per $1000. / $600 Equal to $1000.	Freight per 100 lbs for 50 lbs and upwards.	Special Rates or Remarks.
*Bath,	Ill.	125	175	375
*Berlin,	"	"	"	350
*Broadwell,	"	125	200	350
Bushnell,	"	100	150	350
*Bethalto,	"	100	225	3
*Buda,	"	75	100	275
*Bristol,	"	50	75	175
*Biggsville,	"	100	125	300
*Bardolph,	"	100	150	300
*Barrington,	"	75	150	175
*Blackberry,	"	50	50	75
*Babcock's Grove,	"	50	75	150
*Baileyville,	"	75	75	"
Camp Point,	"	100	125	275
Carlinville,	"	150	225	300
Carthage,	"	100	150	375
* *Catlin,*	"	125	200	"
Centralia,	"	100	150	250
* *Chatham,*	"	150	225	3.
Chicago,	"	75	125	150
Chenoa,	"	100	125	2.
Chilicothe,	"	125	150	250
Charleston,	"	100	175	325
Clinton,	"	100	125	175
* *Colona,*	"	125	150	250
Courtlandt,	"	75	75	100
*Crystal Lake,	"	75	150	175
* *Cerro Gordo,*	"	100	150	250
* *Cruger,*	"	"	"	300

FROM Como Ill TO		Bank Notes per $1000 / $600 Equal to $1000.	Freight per 100 lbs for 50 lbs and upwards.	Special Rates or Remarks.
* *Chatsworth,*	Ill.	100	125	2 50
* *Clayton,*	"	"	"	3.
* *Chandlersville,*	"	125	175	"
*CLINTONVILLE,	"	50	75	1 25
*CLYDE,	"	125	225	2 25
*COMO,	"			x x
*CAREY,	"	75	100	1 75
*CHERRY VALLEY,	"	75	125	2.
*COTTAGE HILL,	"	50	75	1 50
*CHEMUNG,	"	75	125	2 00
*CALEDONIA,	"	"	"	2 25
Canton,	"	125	200	2 75
*CAMERON,	"	75	125	2 00
*COATSBURG,	"	100	175	2 75
*CLIFTON,	"	75	125	2 00
*COLMAR,	"	100	100	2 50
*CENTRAL CITY,	"	100	125	2 50 Closed
*CALUMET,	"	75	125	2.
*COLCHESTER,	"	100	170	2 75
*CHEBANSE,	"	100	100	2.
Danville,	"	125	225	3 75
Decatur,	"	100	125	2 25
DIXON,	"	75	50	50
*DUNLEITH,	"	100	125	2 50
Dwight,	"	125	175	2 00
*DEKALB,	"	50	50	1 00
*DUDLEY,	"	100	125	2 50
*DUNTON,	"	75	100	2 00
*DORSEY'S STATION,	"	100	225	2 50

FROM Como Ill. TO		Bank Notes per $1000. $600 Equal to $1000.	Freight per 100 lbs for 50 lbs and upwards.	Special rates or Remarks.
*DEMENT, ...	Ill.	80	80	100
*DANBY,...........	"	80	70	150
*DESPLAINES, ...	"	70	100	200
*DUNDEE, ...	"	"	"	125
*DAVIS, ...	"	70	70	150
*DAKOTA, ...	"	"	"	"
*DURAND, ...	"	"	"	175
*DALLAS CITY, ...	"	100	225	575
EARL....	"	70	100	100
EFFINGHAM,........	"	75	120	250
ELGIN, ...	"	50	125	150
**Elkhart*,..........	"	100	200	2.
**Elmwood*, ...	"	125	150	250
El Paso, ...	"	100	120	150
**Eureka*, ...	"	100	[illegible]	2.
*EVANSTON,........	"	70	120	2.
*ELROY, ...	"	70	100	150
*EDGEWOOD, ...	"	100	120	275
*ETNA, ...	"	100	180	250
**Fairbury*,.........	"	120	100	150
FREEPORT, ...	"	75	100	1.50
FULTON CITY.......	"	50	50	50
*FRANKLIN GROVE...	"	"	"	75
*FRANKFORT, ...	"	100	100	
*FORRESTON, ...	"	50	50	125
Farmington, ...	"	125	200	300
Galesburgh,......	"	75	125	200
GALENA,...........	"	75	125	175
GALVA, ...	"	75	125	225

FROM Como Ill TO		Bank Notes per $1000. $600 Equal to $1000.	Freight per 100 lbs for 50 lbs and upwards.	Special Rates, or Remarks.
* *Gardner*, ...	Ill.	125	175	225
Geneseo, ...	"	125	150	175
GENEVA, ...	"	75	75	100
GILLESPIE, ...	"	125	225	250
Gilman, ...	"	100	150	175
Girard, ...	"	150	225	300
* *Gridley*, ...	"	100	120	"
* *Gibson*, ...	"	100	130	"
*GARDEN PRAIRIE, ..	"	50	100	175
*GILBERTS, ...	"	75	100	150
Havana, ...	"	125	200	375
Henry, ...	"	125	150	3.
HILLSBORO, ...	"	100	150	3.
Homer, ...	"	100	120	375
*HUDSON, ...	"	"	"	250
*HEYWORTH, ...	"	100	130	230
*HUNTLEY, ...	"	75	100	150
*HALDANE, ...	"	50	50	100
*HARVARD, ...	"	75	100	200
*HEBRON, ...	"	100	150	"
*HARLEM, ...	"	50	75	150
*IRVING, ...	"	100	125	300
* *Illiopolis*, ...	"	100	175	350
Jacksonville, ...	"	125	200	"
Joliet, ...	"	100	175	175
*JUNCTION, ...	"	50	75	125
KANKAKEE, ...	"	75	150	2.
KANSAS, ...	"	100	120	3.
KEWANEE, ...	"	75	125	2 m

FROM Como Ill TO		Bank Notes per $1000. $600 Equal to $1000.	Freight per 100 lbs for 50 lbs and upwards.	Special rates or Remarks.
Knoxville, ...	Ill.	125	150	3.00
*KINMUNDY, ...	"	100	120	3 00
*KAPPA, ...	"	"	"	250
*KANE, ...	"	50	50	1 00
Lacon, ...	"	125	150	3.
LANE, ...	"	50	50	1.00
LaSalle or **Peru**, .	"	75	100	125
Lexington, ...	"	125	175	225
**Lincoln*,..........	"	125	150	200
LITCHFIELD,........	"	100	150	3.
Liverpool, ...	"	125	200	375
Lockport,.........	"	100	175	175
LODA, ...	"	100	150	2.
Lewiston, ...	"			200
*LELAND, ...	"	50	75	200
*LAPRAIRIE, ...	"	100	125	"
*LENA, ...	"	75	100	175
*LAWRENCE, ...	"	100	200	closed
*LODI,.............	"	50	50	125
*LAKE FOREST, ...	"	75	125	200
*LANARK,..........	"	"	"	175
MACOMB,..........	"	100	175	225
MARENGO, ...	"	50	125	150
MATTOON,..........	"	100	175	225
MENDOTA, ...	"	50	75	125
Middleport, ...	"			300
Minooka, ...	"	100	175	200
Mokena, ...	"	100	150	"
Moline,...........	"	125	150	"

FROM Como Ill. TO		Bank Notes per $1,000. $600 Equal to $1000.	Freight per 100 lbs. for 50 lbs. and upwards.	Special Rates or Remarks.
MONMOUTH, ...	Ill.	75	150	200
**Monticello*, ...	"	100	150	225
Morris, ...	"	100	175	225
MORRISON, ...	"	50	50	80
Mt. Sterling, ...	"	100	200	3.
Meradosa, ...	"			"
MOUNT CARROLL, ...	"	75	120	175
*MALTA, ...	"	50	50	100
*MAROA, ...	"	100	175	275
*MINONK, ...	"	100	125	175
*MASON, ...	"	"	"	275
*MONEE, ...	"	75	120	175
*MATTESON, ...	"	"	"	"
*MILTON, ...	"	100	150	200
*MALDEN, ...	"	75	100	"
*MANTENO, ...	"	75	125	200
*MACON, ...	"	100	175	175
*MOAWEQUA, ...	"	100	100	"
**Maynor*, ...	"			100 200
**Marsailles*, ...	"	100	150	225
**McLean*, ...	"	100	125	200
*McHENRY, ...	"	75	150	150
*MAGNOLIA, ...	"	75	175	
**Mechanicsburg*, ...	"	100	120	275
NAPIERVILLE, ...	"	75	100	175
Naples, ...	"	125	200	350
*NEPONSET, ...	"	75	100	225
*NEOGA, ...	"	75	120	200
*NEW RUTLAND, ...	"	50	75	150

FROM Como Ill TO		Bank Notes per $1000. $600 Equal to $1000.	Freight per 100 lbs for 50 lbs and upwards.	Special Rates or Remarks.
**Niantic*, ...	Ill.	100	175	250
**Nilwood*, ...	"	125	200	300
*NACHUSA, ...	"	50	50	75
*NOKOMIS, ...	"	100	125	250
*NORA, ...	"	75	100	175
*NEVADA, Bidott.	"	75	75	"
*NELSON, ...	"	50	50	50
ONARGA,...........	"	100	175	200
Ottawa, ...	"	100	175	225
OKAW, ...	"	100	150	"
*OGLE, ...	"	50	50	75
*ONEIDA, ...	"	50	100	200
*OCONEE,...........	"	100	125	300
*OSWEGO, ...	"	50	75	175
*OQUAWKA JUNCTION,	"	100	125	200
*O*dell*, ...	"	125	150	225
PANA, ...	"	100	125	225
* PANOLA, ...	"	100	100	2.25
PARIS, ...	"	100	175	300
PECATONICA, ...	"	75	100	175
Pekin, ...	"	125	200	300
*PERU, ...	"	50	75	125
Peoria, ...	"	125	150	200
POLO, ...	"	75	75	125
Pontiac, ...	"	125	175	225
PRINCETON, ...	"	75	100	250
Port Byron, ...	"			3.
*PLANO, ...	"	50	75	2'
*PLYMOUTH, ...	"	100	125	300

FROM Como Ill TO		Bank Notes per $1000 — $600 Equal to $1000.	Freight per 100 lbs for 50 lbs and upwards.	Special Rates or Remarks.
*Patoka,	Ill.	100	125	225
●Prairie City,	"			250
*Paxton,	"	75	150	225
*Pera,	"	"	"	"
*Pesotum,	"	100	150	"
*Palatine,	"	75	150	200
Quincy,	"	100	175	250
Richmond,	"	75	150	175
Rockford,	"	75	125	"
Rock Island,	"	125	175	225
**Rome,*	"	125	150	300
*Ridgefield.	"	75	150	175
*Round Grove,	"	50	50	50
*Ringwood,	"	75	150	175
*Roscoe,	"	75	125	175
*Rantoul,	"	75	150	225
*Ramsey,	"	100	125	"
Rosemond,	"	100	100	"
*Sandoval,	"	100	150	225
●Sandwich,	"	75	75	150
Sheffield,	"	125	150	250
Shelbyville,	"	100	150	"
**Shipmans,*	"	150	225	"
Springfield,	"	150	225	"
Sterling,	"	50	50	50
Sycamore,	"	50	50	125
*Scale's Mound	"	50	125	275
*Sandford's,	"	100	150	250
*Sublette,	"	50	75	150

FROM Como Ill TO		Bank Notes per $1000. $600 Equal to $1000.	Freight per 100 lbs for 50 lbs and upwards.	Special Rates or Remarks.
*SHANNON, ...	Ill.	75	125	175
*SOMONAUK, ...	"	50	75	200
*ST. AUGUSTINE, ...	"	100	150	275
**Sadorus*, ...	"	100	175	350
**Secor*, ...	"	100	150	300
**Seneca*, ...	"	"	"	225
**Summit*, ...	"	100	100	175
**Sidney*, ...	"	100	125	375
Tiskilwa, ...	"	125	150	200
Tolono, ...	"	100	175	225
*TONICA, ...	"	100	100	150
**Trenton*, ...	"	125	100	"
TUSCOLA, ...	"	100	150	225
*TENNESSEE, ...	"	"	"	250
*THORNTON, ...	"	75	125	175
*TONTI, ...	"	100	125	275
**Towanda*, ...	"	"	"	250
*UNION, ...	"	50	50	150
URBANA or CHAMPAIGNE.	"	75	175	225
*UNION GROVE, ...	"	50	150	50
**Utica*, ...	"	50	75	200
VANDALIA, ...	"	100	150	225
Virden, ...	"	150	225	300
**Virginia*, ...	"	125	175	375
WARREN, ...	"	75	125	200
WARSAW, ...	"	100	225	350
**Washington*, ...	"	125	150	3.
WAUKEGAN, ...	"	75	150	200
WHEATON, ...	"	50	100	125

FROM Como Ill TO		Bank Notes per $1000 — $600 Equal to $1000.	Freight per 100 lbs for 50 lbs and upwards.	Special Rates or Remarks.	
Williamsville, ...	Ill.	125	150		225
Wilmington, ...	"	125	175		200
WINDSOR, ...	"	100	125		250
WOODSTOCK, ...	"	75	150		2
*WOOSUNG, ...	"	50	50		125
*WATAGA, ...	"	50	100		2.
*WAPELLA, ...	"	100	150		250
*WYANETT, ...	"	75	100		"
*WATSON, ...	"	100	125		200
*WINNEBAGO, ...	"	50	75		175
*WAYNE, ...	"	"	"		125
*WINFIELD, ...	"	"	"		"
WENONA, ...	"	50	75		275
*YOUNG AMERICA, ...	"	75	125		200
**Yates City,*	"	50	100		275
* [illegible]	"	100	150		300
* [illegible]	"	100	100	125	200
[illegible]	"	75	125		200
[illegible]	"	100	200		275
* [illegible]	"	100	150	100	200
Poplar Grove	"	75	125		175
Paxton	"	100	150		225
Malden	"	75	100		175
Tower Hill	"	100	150		300
Apple River	"	75	125		200
Lena	"	75	125		175
Meriden	"	50	75	75	225
Farina				150	300
Lostant				125	250

FROM Como Ill TO	Bank Notes per $1000. $600 Equal to $1000.	Freight per 100 lbs for 50 lbs and upwards.	Special rates or Remarks.
Rock City	125	200	
Rockton	125	"	
Peotone	100	"	
Keokuk Junc	125	250	
Fowler	"	300	
Capron	100	175	
Berkley	150	200	
Montgomery	100	200	
Shabbona	125	3.00	
Bush Hill (Hinsdale)			
Lyons	125	200	
Downers Grove	"	"	
Palmyra	125	350	
Dorchester	"	300	
Alum	150	"	
Hinsdale	100	200	
Odine	150	3.00	
Sigel	125	250	
Lisle	100	200	
Alden	"	200	
Thompson	125	300	
Council Hill	100	200	
Normal	125	250	

FROM Como Ill TO	Bank Notes per $1000. $600 Equal to $1000.	Freight per 100 lbs for 50 lbs and upwards.	Special Rates, or Remarks.
Appleton, ... Wis.	100	225	300
*Arena, ... "	75	225	"
*Avoca, ... "	100	200	"
*Allen's Grove, ... "	"	"	225
*Afton, ... "	75	125	200
Beaver Dam, ... "	75	200	300
Beloit, ... "	75	125	200
Berlin, ... "	100	250	350
Broadhead, ... "	100	175	250
Boscobel, ... "			125 300
Burlington, ... "			100 300
*Black Earth, ... "	75	225	275
*Bangor, ... "	175	250	350
*Brandon, ... "	75	175	300
*Burnett Junction,. "	"	"	275
Clinton, ... "	100	200	225
Columbus, ... "	100	225	275
*Cambria, ... "	75	200	325
*Calamine, ... "	100	150	3.
*Chester, ... "	75	175	275
*Cassville, ... "	125	275	250
*Cross Plains, ... "	75	225	300
Delevan, ... "	75	175	225
*Darlington, ... "	100	150	200
*Darien, ... "	75	150	225
*Deansvile, ... "	100	200	275
*De Soto, ... "	175	250	425
*Delaware, ... "			150 350
Elkhorn, ... "	75	200	250

FROM *Como Ill*

TO

Margin note	TO		Bank Notes per $1000. $600 Equal to $1000.	Freight per 100 lbs for 50 lbs and upwards.	Special rates or Remarks.	
W S	*Eagle, ...	Wis.	75	175		250
	Fond Du Lac, ...	"	75	225		200
W S	*Fulton, ...	"	75	175		250
	Fox Lake, ...	"	75	200		3.
	Geneva, .. *Closed*	"	75	175		
	Green Bay, ...	"	100	250		350
W S	*Genesee, ...	"	75	175		250
	*Greenfield, ...	"	100	200		325
	*Genoa, ...	"	75	125		225
	Horicon, ...	"	75	200		275
	*Hartland, ...	"	75	175		225
	*Hartford, ...	"	"	"		3.
Marshall	*Hanchettsville, ...	"	100	200		275
	*Iron Bridge, ...	"	75	175		"
	Janesville, ...	"	75	150		225
	Jefferson, ...	"	75	175		250
	*Juneau, ...	"	"	"		"
W S	*Juda, ...	"	100	175		"
	Kenosha, ...	"	75	150		200
	Kilbourn City, ...	"	125	250		300
	LaCrosse, ...	"	~~[illegible]~~	~~[illegible]~~	125	375
W S	Lone Rock, ...	"				300
	*Lowell, ...	"	100	200		275
	Madison, ...	"	75	200		225
W S	Mazo Manie, ...	"	75	250		3.
	Menasha, ...	"	75	250		"
	*Milton, ...	"	75	200		250
	Milwaukee, ...	"	75	175		2.
	Mineral Point, ...	"	100	150		2.25

	FROM Como Ill TO		Bank Notes per $1,000. $600 Equal to $1000.	Freight per 100 lbs. for 50 lbs. and upwards.	Special Rates or Remarks.
U.S	MONROE, ...	Wis.	100	175	250
"	*MUSCODA, ...	"			350
"	*MCFARLAND, ...	"	75	175	250
	*MAUSTON, ...	"	75	200	325
	*MINN. JUNCTION, ...	"	75	175	275
	*MANITOWOC, ...	"	100	200	425
	NEW LISBON, ...	"	75	200	325
U.S	*NORTH PRAIRIE, ...	"	75	175	250
	*NEWPORT, ...	"	125	250	300
	*NEENAH, ...	"	75	225	"
	OCONOMOWOC, ...	"	75	200	250
	OSHKOSH, ...	"	75	225	275
	*OAKFIELD, ...	"	75	200	"
U.S	*OXFORD, ...	"	100	175	250
	PORTAGE CITY, ...	"	75	225	300
	PRAIRIE DU CHIEN, .	"	125	300	350
	*PINE LAKE, ...	"	75	175	250
	*PEWAUKEE, ...	"	"	"	225
U.S	*PALMYRA, ...	"	"	"	250
	*PORT WASHINGTON, .	"	100	200	400
	RACINE, ...	"	75	175	200
	RIPON, ...	"	75	200	325
	*ROLLING PRAIRIE ...	"	75	175	3.
	*~~ROCKTON~~, ...	"	75	125	
	*RANDOLPH, ...	"	75	200	325
	*RUBICON, ...	"	75	175	250
	*RICHFIELD, ...	"	"	"	225
	*~~ROCK RUN~~, ...	"	75	75	
	SHEBOYGAN, ...	"			125 400

FROM Como Ill TO	Bank Notes per \$1000. — \$600 Equal to \$1000.	Freight per 100 lbs for 50 lbs and upwards.	Special Rates or Remarks.
Sparta, ... Wis.	150	250	350
Stoughton, ... "	75	175	250
Sun Prairie, ... "	100	200	275
*Spring Green, ... "			300
*Shopier, ... "	75	125	225
*Springfield, ... "	75	175	250
*Schleisengerville, "	"	"	225
*Sharon, ... "	100	200	"
*Salem, I. & n. R. R. Rd "	75	125	225
*Sheboygan Falls, .. "			125 4.
*Tomah, ... "	150	250	325
*Two Rivers, ... "			125 4.
*Union Grove, ... "			" 250
Watertown, ... "	75	200	"
Waukesha, ... "	75	200	"
Waupun, ... "	75	200	3.
Whitewater, ... "	75	200	250
Woodland, ... "	75	175	"
*Waterloo, ... "	100	200	275
*Wauzeka, ... "	125	275	350
*Waukau, ... "	100	200	"
[illegible]	75	125	225
*[illegible]	75	200	325
*[illegible]	175	250	350
[illegible]	75	175	350
Cambria ..	75	225	325
Randolph ..	75	225	325
Magnolia ..	75	125	225
Woodman		-	150 3.50

FROM Como Ill TO	Bank Notes per $1000 — $600 Equal to $1000.	Freight per 100 lbs for 50 lbs and upwards.	Special Rates or Remarks.
Eau Claire	375	7.75	
Ft Atkinson	100	250	
Glenbulah	125	400	
Hudson	200	600	
Kaukauna	150	350	
Midland	125	325	
Manitowoc	"	425	
Prescott	200	625	
Clyman	125	250	
Riverside	"	2.	
Footville	"	225	
Wrightstown	175	350	
Oregon	125	225	
Durand	300	750	
Evansville	125	225	
Lyndon	"	325	
Plymouth	"	4.	
Alma	250	550	
Trempeleau	"	5.00	
Wyocena	150	300	
Bristol	125	225	
Florence	"	250	
Fountain City	200	475	
Pewaukee	250	425	
Peshtigo	"	"	
Oconto	"	"	
Omro	125	350	
Mossakunnee	250	425	
Rio	125	300	

Continued on Page 129

o Bill to Mukwonago

-o- " " Portage City

FROM Como Ill TO

FROM / TO	Bank Notes per $1000. $600 Equal to $1000.	Freight per 100 lbs for 50 lbs and upwards.	Special Rates or Remarks.
Brownsville, ... Minn.	150	300	
Belle Plaine	275	500	
Chatfield	3.	425	
Faribault	"	6.	
Hastings	"	375	
Henderson	"	575	
Lake City	225	375	
La Sueur.	300	575	
Mankato	"	650	
Wilton	"	"	
Mantorville	275	450	
Northfield	300	575	
Reeds Landing	225	375	
Red Wing	"	"	
Rochester	"	400	
Stillwater	250	"	
St Paul	"	375	
St Charles	225	400	
St Peter	300	675	
Shakopee	275	475	
Wabashaw	225	375	
Winona	200	350	
Minneiska	"	375	
Waseca	275	450	
Owatonna	300	525	

FROM Como Ill TO	Bank Notes per $1000 / $600 Equal to $1000.	Freight per 100 lbs for 50 lbs and upwards.	Special Rates or Remarks.
AGENCY CITY, ... Iowa.	175	250	350
ANAMOSA, ...	125	200	250
*Atalissa, ... "	150	200	Bill to Ottumwa
Adell, ... "	325	650	825
Burlington, ... "	100	125	250
*BATAVIA, ... "	175	250	300
*Bentonsport, ... "	150	275	" 350 Keokuk
Brooklyn, ... "	325	600	" " Ottumwa
CEDAR FALLS, ... "	150	225	300
Cedar Rapids, ... "	125	150	200
CLINTON, ... "	75	50	100
*CAMANCHE, ... "	70	100	125
*CLAYTON, ... "	125	275	250
*CLARENCE OR ONION GROVE, "	120	150	1[illegible]
Council Bluffs, ... "	350	470	" 900 St Joseph
Columbus City, ... "	150	270	" " Muscatine
Davenport, ... "	125	175	250
*DANVILLE, ... "	75	175	250
DEWITT, ... "	70	100	150
DUBUQUE, ... "	75	125	225
*Durant, ... "	100	200	275
*DYERSVILLE, ... "	125	175	300
Des Moines, ... "	300	550	" 600 Ottumwa
*EPWORTH, ... "	100	150	300
*EARLVILLE, ... "	100	175	325
Eddyville, ... "	225	300	" " Ottumwa
FAIRFIELD, ... "	150	250	300
FORT MADISON, ... "	"	"	325
*FARLEY, ... "	"	175	3..

FROM Como Ill. TO	Bank Notes per $1000. — $600 Equal to $1000.	Freight per 100 lbs for 50 lbs and upwards.	Special rates or Remarks.
Farmington, ...Iowa.	[illegible]	[illegible]	See [illegible] 450
**Fontinell,*.......... "	350	450	" " 875
**Fulton,*............ "	100	100	300
*GUTTENBURG, ... "	150	250	250
*GLENDALE, ... "	100	200	300
Glenwood, ... "	350	400	" " [illegible]
Grinnell, ... "	200	300	" " 500
**Homestead,* .... "	100	250	375
INDEPENDENCE, ... "	120	200	350
Iowa City, ... "	125	200	325
*JESSUP,............ "	100	200	300
Keokuk,.......... "	100	225	325
LYONS, ... "	75	50	100
*LANSING, ... "	150	200	275
*LOUDON,........... "	120	100	175
*LISBON,............ "	"	"	200
*LEGRAND, ... "	150	200	275
Lewis,............ "	400	600	Bill to [illegible]
MARION, ... "	120	200	Place 275
MT. PLEASANT, ... "	125	175	"
*MECHANICSVILLE. ... "	120	100	200
~~*MIDLAND,~~.......... "			
*MT. VERNON. ...... "	120	100	200
•MANCHESTER, ... "	125	170	200 325
*MONTICELLO,....... "	120	200	"
*MCGREGOR, ... "	150	200	[illegible] 275
MARSHALL, ... "	"	"	275
Muscatine,......... "	100	200	375
**Moscow,* .... "	100	100	"

FROM Como Ills TO	Bank Notes per $1000. $600 Equal to $1000.	Freight per 100 lbs for 50 lbs and upwards.	Special Rates, or Remarks.
Marengo, ...Iowa.	150	275	Bill to Pella 375
*MONTROSE, ... "	150	200	325
*NOTTINGHAM, ... "	125	200	Closed
*NEW LONDON,...... "	70	175	275
Newton, ... "	225	375	" " 525 Pella
*ONION GROVE OR CLARENCE, "	125	200	See Clarence
Ottumwa, ... "	175	200	300
*OTTER CREEK, ... "	100	200	Closed
Ononwa, ... "	100	275	325
Oskaloosa, ... "	250	350	" " 500 Ottumwa
Pella, ... "	270	450	" 625 "
*ROME, ... "	175	250	300
*SAND SPRING, ... "	125	200	250
**Sidney*, ... "	325	425	675 Council [illegible]
**Summit*, ... "	100	125	" " 350 Pella
TOLEDO, ... "	150	200	250
~~*VERMILLION, ... "~~			
WATERLOO, ... "	150	225	350
West Liberty,...... "	150	250	325
Wilton, ... "	125	200	"
*WINTHROP, ... "	125	200	350
*WORTHINGTON,..... "	"	"	250
*WHEATLAND,....... "	125	150	Bill to [illegible]
* *Wiscotta*, ... "	300	550	750
* *Walcott*,........... "	100	175	275
Washington, ... "	150	275	" " 400 Pella
Winterset, ... "	325	650	" " 875 [illegible]
*YANKEE RUN, or WHEAT-LAND, ... "	See Wheatland		Bill Office 125

FROM Como Ill TO	Bank Notes per $1000. / $600 Equal to $1000.	Freight per 100 lbs for 50 lbs and upwards.	Special rates or Remarks.
[illegible]	125	200	300
[illegible]	"	"	300
[illegible]	150	200	250
	"	"	"
[illegible]			
Fort Dodge	250	500	
Sioux City "	400	975	
Buck Eye	100	225	225
Low Moor [?]	75	150	
Nevada	175	3.	
Ackley	"	450	
Peosta [?]	125	3.	
Marysville [?]	"	325	
Webster City	2.	475	
Ft Dodge	275	950	
Sioux City	450	11.25	
Alden	175	450	
Norway	125	250 [?]	
Langworthy	100	3.	
[illegible]	125	250	
Chelsea	"	"	
Fairfax	100	"	
Sabula	"	200	
Iowa Falls	175	450	
Springville	100	3.	
Oxford	150	"	
Waverly	"	325	
Janesville	"	"	
State Center	175	300	

Continued on page 106

FROM Como Ill TO	Bank Notes per $1,000. $600 Equal to $1000.	Freight per 100 lbs. for 50 lbs. and upwards.	Special Rates or Remarks.
*ALEXANDRIA, ... Mo.	100	225	325
Allen, ... "	225	350	Bill [illegible]
Arrow Rock, ... "	275	400	" [illegible]
Berlin, ... "	300	450	" [illegible]
Boonville, ... "	270	425	" 500
**Brunswick,* .... "	350	500	" [illegible]
*BEVIER, ... "	170	270	450
*BROOKFIELD, ... "	"	"	475
*BRECKENRIDGE, ... "	200	325	525
*BUCKLIN, ... "	170	275	450
*CAMERON, ... "	200	300	525
CHILLICOTHE, ... "	"	"	475
*CLARENCE, ... "	170	250	4.
*CANTON, ... "	100	225	325
*CLARKSVILLE, ... "	"	"	"
*CARBON, ... "	170	270	375
*CALLAO, ... "	"	"	450
Cambridge, ... "	270	400	Bill [illegible]
Centralia, ... "	250	350	" " [illegible]
California, ... "	270	350	" " [illegible]
Columbia, ... "	270	400	" " [illegible]
Camden, ... "	300	450	" " 600
Chamois, ... "	200	325	" " 375
Franklin, ... "	170	300	" " 350
Florence, ... "	275	370	" " [illegible]
**Forest City,* ..... "	200	400	" " [illegible]
Fulton, ... "	225	420	" " [illegible]
**Georgetown,* ...... "	270	425	" " 6.
Gasconade, ... "	250	325	" " 375

FROM Como Ill TO		Bank Notes per $1000. $600 Equal to $1000.	Freight per 100 lbs for 50 lbs and upwards.	Special Rates or Remarks.
Glasgow, ...	Mo.	270	420	B. ell St. Louis 575
Hannibal, ...	"	100	225	325
*HUNNEWELL, ...	"	100	220	350
*HAMILTON, ...	"	200	300	5.
High Hill, ...	"	270	370	B. ell Macon City
Hermann, ...	"	200	320	" St. Louis
Hill's Landing	"	300	300	" St. Joseph 7
Independence, ...	"	300	425	" 625
Iatan, ...	"	250	400	" 6.
Jefferson City, ...	"	200	320	" St. Louis 375
Jacksonville, ...	"	200	325	" M. City 450
~~*Junction City,* ....~~	"			—
KIDDER, ...	"	175	275	450
Kansas City, ...	"	275	425	" St. Joseph 625
Knob Noster, ...	"	350	775	" 1075
LACLEDE, ...	"	175	275	475
*LAGRANGE, ...	"	100	220	325
*LOUISIANA, ...	"	"	"	"
Lexington, ...	"	300	450	" St. Joseph 650
Liberty Landing, ...	"	300	425	" 625
Macon City, ...	"	175	275	425
Mexico, ...	"	275	350	" M. City 475
Miller's Landing, ..	"	175	300	" St. Louis 350
Miami, ...	"	350	470	" St. Joseph 7
Marshall, ...	"	350	620	" 875
**Martinsburg,*	"	270	300	" M. City 475
**Missouri City,*	"	300	420	" St. Joseph 620
Montgomery, ...	"	270	350	" St. Louis 475
*OSBORN, ...	"	200	320	525

FROM Como Ill TO		Bank Notes per $1000 / $600 Equal to $1000.	Freight per 100 lbs for 50 lbs and upwards.	Special Rates or Remarks.
* *Oregon*, ...	Mo.	300	400	Do 600
Osage,.............	"	200	350	" 375
Otterville,..........	"	220	350	" 400
PALMYRA,..........	"	100	225	3.
* *Providence*, ...	"	275	350	" 6
Pleasant Hill,......	"	350	575	" 825
* *Parkville*,..........	"	270	400	" 625
* *Rocheport*, ...	"	300	520	" 700
* *Renick*,............	"	250	325	" 375
SHELBINA, ...	"	170	200	"
*STOCKTON, ...	"	170	275	450
*ST. CATHARINES,....	"	"	"	475
*STEWARTSVILLE,....	"	200	325	525
Sedalia, ...	"	220	350	" 4,00
Smithton,..........	"	"	"	" "
Savannah, ...	"			575
Syracuse, ...	"	250	375	" [illegible]
St. Aubert, ...	"	200	325	" 375
St. Charles, ...	"	150	255	" 450
Sturgeon, ...	"	250	350	" "
St. Joseph, ...	"	200	325	550
St. Louis, ...	"	150	225	3,00
Tipton, ...	"	225	350	" 4.
UTICA, ...	"	200	300	5.
Warrenton, ...	"	270	370	" "
Washington, ...	"	170	300	" 350
Wellsville, ...	"	[illegible]	[illegible]	500
Waverly, ...	"	350	470	" 625
Wellsburg,.........	"	270	370	" [illegible]

FROM Como Ill TO	Bank Notes per $1000. / $600 Equal to $1000.	Freight per 100 lbs for 50 lbs and upwards.	Special Rates or Remarks.
Wellington, ... Mo.	350	475	Bill St Joseph [illegible]
Wentzville, ... "	275	375	" [illegible] City
Weston, ... "	250	400	" St Joseph [illegible]
Westport, ... "	300	450	" 650
Warrensburg, ... "	275	425	" St Louis [illegible]
Wright City. ...... "	200	300	" 625
W S Sonora "	300	425	" St Joseph
x Bottsville	225	475	
x Monroe "	200	350	
x Morrisville "	250	500	
New Haven			

FROM Como TO	Bank Notes per $1000 — $600 Equal to $1000.	Freight per 100 lbs for 50 lbs and upwards.	Special Rates or Remarks.
*Ashland, ... Kan.	400	800	11.00
Atchison, ... "	250	400	6
*Doniphan, ... "	"	"	"
*Fort Ripley, ... "	400	900	12.25
Indianola, ... "	350	700	9.75
Iowa Point, ... "	300	400	6.
Junction City, ... "	400	900	12.25
Lawrence .... "	300	525	8.75
Lecompton, ... "	300	575	8.25
Leavenworth, ... "	250	400	7
Manhattan, ... "	400	700	10.25
Ogden, ... "	"	800	11.50
*Quindaro, ... "	275	425	6.25
Rushville, ... "	250	400	6
*Sonora, ... "			
Sidney Landing, ... "	300	425	6.25
*Sumner, ... "	250	400	6.
*Tecumseh, ... "	325	575	8.25
Topeka, ... "	"	"	10.
Wyandot, ... "	275	425	8.75
White Cloud, ... "	300	400	6.
[illegible]	400	900	

FROM Como Ill TO	Bank Notes per $1000. $600 Equal to $1000.	Freight per 100 lbs for 50 lbs and upwards.	Special rates or Remarks.
New Hartford Io	125	375	Ft Dodge
Boonsboro	"	300	
Marshall	100	200	
Colo	200	300	
Grand Mound	75	150	
Ames	200	325	
Applington	"	450	Iowa Falls
Boone	150	300	Boonsboro
Tipton	125	225	
Calamus	100	200	
Panora	275	550	C Bluff
Lewis	325	825	"

FROM Como Ill TO	Bank Notes per $1000. / $600 Equal to $1000.	Freight per 100 lbs for 50 lbs and upwards.	Special Rates or Remarks.
Brownsville, ...Neb.	3 50	4 20	6 25
**Bellevue,* .... "	"	4 75	7.
Columbus, ... "	6 00	12 25	16.25
Elkhorn, ... "	4 00	9 75	13.25
Fremont, ... "	"	10 75	24 50
Ft. Kearney, ... "	6 00	12 75	17.
**Nemaha,* .... "	3 50	4 20	6 25
Nebraska City, ... "	"	"	"
Omaha, ... "	"	4 75	3 50 9 00
Plattsmouth, ... "	"	"	7 00

TARIFF OF RATES FROM BUFFALO OR SUSPENSION BRIDGE

TO		Bank Notes per $1000. $600 Equal to $1000.	Freight per 100 lbs for 50 lbs and upwards.	Special Rates or Remarks.
ALBANY, (*Local rate*,)	N. Y.	.75	1.50	
AMSTERDAM, ...	"	"	"	
ALDER CREEK, ...	"	.63	1.38	
ALBION, Oswego Co.,	"	.75	1.50	
ADAMS, ...	"	"	"	
ADAMS CENTRE, ...	"	"	"	
ANTWERP, ...	"	1.00	1.75	
AUBURN, ...	"	.50	.87	
AURORA, ...	"	"	1.00	
AKRON, ...	"	"	.75	
ALEXANDER, ...	"	.38	.38	
ATTICA, ...	"	"	.50	
ADAMS BASIN, ...	"	.50	.75	
ALBION, Orleans Co.,	"	"	"	
ADDISON, ...	"	75	1.25	
ALMOND, ...	"	"	1.00	
ALFRED, ...	"	"	"	
ANDOVER, ...	"	"	1.25	
ALLEGHANY, ...	"	"	"	
APULIA, ...	"	"	1.50	
AVON, ...	"	.38	.50	
ALDEN, ...	"	"	.38	
AVOCA, ...	"	.50	.75	
ASHVILLE, ...	"	.75	1.38	

Tariff of rates from Buffalo or Suspension Bridge, to	Bank Notes per $1,000. / $600 Equal to $1000.	Freight per 100 lbs. for 50 lbs. and upwards.	Special Rates or Remarks.
BARRYTOWN, ...N. Y.	.75	2.00	
BOONVILLE, ... "	.63	1.38	
BROWNSVILLE,...... "	1.00	1.75	
BALDWINSVILLE, ... "	.50	1.00	
BIG STREAM, ... "	"	.87	
BERGEN, ...,.. "	.38	.50	
BYRON, ... "	"	"	
BATAVIA, ... "	"	"	
BROCKPORT,........ "	.50	.75	
BINGHAMPTON, ... "	.75	1.25	
BARTON, ... "	"	1.00	
BELVIDERE, ... "	"	1.25	
BATH, ... "	"	.88	
BLOODS, ... "	"	.75	
BURNS, ... "	"	.63	

Tariff of Rates from Buffalo or Suspension Bridge to	Bank Notes per $1000. $600 Equal to $1000.	Freight per 100 lbs for 50 lbs and upwards.	Special Rates, or Remarks.
CRUGERS, ...N. Y.	.75	2.00	
CROTON, ... "	"	"	
COLD SPRING, ... "	"	"	
CARTHAGE, ... "	"	"	
CATSKILL, ... "	"	"	
COXSACKIE, ... "	"	"	
CASTLETON, ... "	"	"	
CRANES VILLAGE, .. "	"	1.50	
COOPERSTOWN, ... "	"	"	
CHERRY VALLEY, ... "	"	"	
CAMDEN, ... "	"	"	
CENTREVILLE, ... "	"	"	
CANTON, St. Lau. Co., "	1.00	1.75	
CANTON, Onond Co., "	.50	.88	
CAPE VINCENT, ... "	1.00	1.75	
CANASTOTA, ... "	.63	1.25	
CHITTENANGO, ... "	"	"	
CAMILLUS, ... "	.50	.87	
CAYUGA BRIDGE, ... "	"	"	
CLIFTON SPRINGS, ... "	"	"	
CLYDE, ... "	"	"	
CHARLOTTE, ... "	.38	.63	
CHURCHVILLE, ... "	"	.50	
CORFU, ... "	"	"	
CHATHAM CENTRE, .. "	1.50	2.00	
CHATHAM 4 CORNERS "	"	"	
CANAAN, ... "	"	"	
CHILI, ... "	.38	.50	
CALEDONIA, ... "	.50	.63	

Tariff of Rates from Buffalo or Suspension Bridge to	Bank Notes per $1000 — $600 Equal to $1000.	Freight per 100 lbs. for 50 lbs. and upwards.	Special Rates or Remarks.
CHASEMONT, ...N. Y.	1.00	1.75	
CHESTER, ... "	1.50	2.25	
COCHECTON, ... "	1.00	1.50	
CALLICOON, ... "	"	"	
CAMPVILLE, ... "	"	1.25	
CHEMUNG, ... "	"	1.00	
CORNING, ... "	.75	"	
CAMERON, ... "	1.00	1.00	
CANISTEO, ... "	"	"	
CUBA, ... "	"	1.25	
CARROLLTON, ... "	"	1.38	
CATTARAUGUS, ... "	.75	"	
CRAIGVILLE, ... "	.75	1.75	
CHESTERVILLE, ... "	"	"	
CHENANGO FORKS, .. "	"	1.50	
COURTLAND, ... "	"	"	
CANDOR CENTRE, ... "	"	1.25	
CANANDAIGUA, ... "	.50	.63	
CAMPBELL, ... "	.75	1.00	
CALEDONIA, ... "	"	.50	
CONESUS, ... "	"	"	
CUYLERVILLE, ... "	.38	"	
CANASERAGA, ... "	1.00	.63	
CASTILE, ... "	.88	.50	

Tariff of Rates from Buffalo or Suspension Bridge to	Bank Notes per $1000. $600 Equal to $1000.	Freight per 100 lbs for 50 lbs and upwards.	Special rates or Remarks.
Dobb's Ferry, ... N. Y.	.75	2.00	
DeKalb, ... "	1.00	1.75	
Deposit, ... "	.75	1.38	
Dayton, ... "	"	"	
Darien, ... "	.38	.38	
Evans Mills, ... N. Y.	1.00	1.75	
Elmira, ... "	.75	1.00	
East Bloomfild, ... "	.50	.63	
East Chatham, ... "	1.50	2.00	

Tariff of Rates from Buffalo or Suspension Bridge to	Bank Notes per $1000 — $600 Equal to $1000.	Freight per 100 lbs for 50 lbs and upwards.	Special Rates or Remarks.
Fishkill, ... N. Y.	.75	2.00	
Fonda, ... "	"	1.50	
Fort Plain, ... "	"	"	
Frankfort, ... "	"	"	
Fulton, ... "	.50	1.00	
Fishers, ... "	"	.75	
Fairport, ... "	"	.87	
Frog Point, ... "	"	1.00	
Ft. Montgomery, .. "	.75	2.00	
Friendship, ... "	"	1.25	
Forrestville, ... "	"	1.50	
Germantown, ... N. Y.	.75	2.00	
Gouverneur, ... "	1.00	1.75	
Geneva, ... "	.50	.87	
Gasport, ... "	"	.75	
Goshen, ... "	.75	1.75	
Genesee, ... "	"	1.25	
Great Valley, ... "	"	1.37	
Gorham, ... "	"	1.50	
Geneseo, ... "	"	.50	
Gainsville, ... "	"	"	

Tariff of Rates from Buffalo or Suspension Bridge, to	Bank Notes per $1000. — $600 Equal to $1000.	Freight per 100 lbs for 50 lbs and upwards.	Special rates or Remarks.
Hudson, ...N. Y.	.75	2.00	
Hyde Park, ... "	"	"	
Hastings, ... "	"	"	
Herkimer,......... "	"	1.50	
Holland Patent, .. "	.63	1.38	
Holley,........... "	.50	.75	
Hoffman's Ferry,.. "	.75	1.50	
Honeoye Falls,.... "	.50	.63	
Herman, ... "	1.00	1.75	
Hawkins, ... "	.75	1.50	
Hancock, ... "	"	1.37	
Hornellsville, ... "	"	.75	
Hinesdale, ... "	"	1.25	
Homer,............ "	"	1.50	
Horse Heads,...... "	"	1.25	
Havana,........... "	"	1.37	
Himrods, ... "	"	1.50	
Irvington, ...N. Y.	.75	2.00	
Ilion, ... "	"	1.50	
Ithica, ... "	.50	1.00	

Tariff of Rates from Buffalo or Suspension Bridge to	Bank Notes per $1000. $600 Equal to $1000.	Freight per 100 lbs for 50 lbs and upwards.	Special Rates, or Remarks.
Jordan, ...N. Y.	.50	1.00	
Knowlsville, ...N. Y.	.50	.75	
Kingston, ... "	.75	2.00	
Kinderhook, ... "	"	"	
Kasoag, ... "	"	1.50	
King's Ferry, ... "	.50	.87	
Kirkville, ... "	.63	1.25	
Keenes, ... "	1.00	1.75	
Kirkwood, ... "	.75	1.25	
Kennedy, ... "	"	"	
Kidder's Ferry, ... "	.50	.88	
Little Falls, ...N. Y.	.75	1.50	
Lamsons, ... "	.50	1.00	
Lavanna, ... "	"	.87	
Lake Ridge, ... "	"	"	
Lodi, ... "	.75	1.00	
Lyons, ... "	.50	.87	
Lancaster, ... "	.38	.50	

Tariff of Rates from Buffalo or Suspension Bridge to	Bank Notes per $1000. — $600 Equal to $1000.	Freight per 100 lbs for 50 lbs and upwards.	Special Rates or Remarks.
Lockport, ...N. Y.	.50	.50	
Limerick, ... "	1.00	1.75	
Le Roy, ... "	.50	.63	
Lordville, ... "	.75	1.50	
Little Valley, ... "	"	1.37	
Lisle, ... "	"	1.50	
Liberty, ... "	"	.75	
Livonia, ... "	"	.50	
Linden, ... "	.38	"	
McConnellsville, N. Y.	.75	1.50	
Mannsville, ... "	"	"	
Manlius, ... "	.63	1.25	
Marcellus, ... "	.50	.87	
Miller's Corners, . "	"	"	
Macedon, ... "	"	"	
Murray, ... "	"	.75	
Middleport, ... "	"	"	
Milton Ferry, ... "	.75	2.00	
Medina, ... "	.50	.75	
Minetto, ... "	"	1.00	
Monroe, ... "	.75	1.75	

Tariff of rates from Buffalo or Suspension Bridge, to	Bank Notes per $1,000. — $600 Equal to $1000.	Freight per 100 lbs. for 50 lbs. and upwards.	Special Rates or Remarks.
Middletown, ... N. Y.	.75	1.70	
Marathon, ... "	"	1.50	
Millport, ... "	"	1.25	
Mount Morris, ... "	.38	.50	
Memphis, ... "	.50	.88	
New York City (Local Rate.) N. Y.	.75	2.00	
Newburgh, ... "	"	"	
New Hamburgh, ... "	"	"	
Newark, ... "	.50	.87	
Narrowsburgh, ... "	.75	1.50	
Nunda, ... "	"	.50	

Tariff of Rates from Buffalo or Suspension Bridge to		Bank Notes per $1000. $600 Equal to $1000.	Freight per 100 lbs for 50 lbs and upwards.	Special Rates or Remarks.
Oriskany, ...	N. Y.	.63	1.25	
Ogdensburgh, ...	"	1.00	1.75	
Oneida, ...	"	.63	1.25	
Oswego, ...	"	.50	1.00	
Ovid, ...	"	.75	"	
Otisville, ...	"	"	1.75	
Owego, ...	"	"	1.25	
Olean, ...	"	"	"	
Peekskill, ...	N. Y.	.75	2.00	
Poughkeepsie, ...	"	"	"	
Palatine Bridge, ..	"	"	1.50	
Prospect, ...	"	.63	1.38	
Pierrepont Manor,	"	.75	1.50	
Philadelphia, ...	"	1.00	1.75	
Potsdam, ...	"	"	"	
Potsdam Junction,	"	"	"	
Parmers, ...	"	.50	1.00	
Pittsford, ...	"	"	.75	
Port Byron, ...	"	"	1.00	
Palmyra, ...	"	"	.87	
Pekin, ...	"	"	.50	

Tariff of Rates from Buffalo or Suspension Bridge to		Bank Notes per $1000 / $600 Equal to $1000.	Freight per 100 lbs for 50 lbs and upwards.	Special Rates or Remarks.
Phelps, ...	N. Y.	.50	.87	
Port Jervis, ...	"	.75	1.50	
Painted Post,.....	"	.50	1.00	
Phillipsville, ...	"	.75	1.25	
Perrysburgh, ...	"	"	1.37	
Penn Yan, ...	"	"	1.50	
Preble, ...	"	"	"	
Portage, ...	"	"	.50	
Panama,...........	"	"	1.50	
Pulaski, ...	"	"	"	
Pembroke, ...	"	.38	.50	
Richland, ...	N. Y.	.75	1.50	
Rondout,..........	"	"	2.00	
Rhinebeck,........	"	"	"	
Remsen, ...	"	.63	1.38	
Rome, ...	"	"	1.25	
Richville,.........	"	1.00	1.75	
Rathboneville,....	"	.75	1.25	
Rochester,........	"	.38	.50	
Randolph, ...	"	.75	1.00	

Tariff of Rates from Buffalo or Suspension Bridge to	Bank Notes per $1000. — $600 Equal to $1000.	Freight per 100 lbs for 50 lbs and upwards.	Special rates or Remarks.
SCARBOROUGH,......N. Y.	.75	2.00	
SING SING, ... "	"	"	
SPUYTEN DUYVIL, .. "	"	"	
STATTSBURG, ... "	"	"	
SAUGERTIES, ... "	"	"	
STUYVESANT, ... "	"	"	
SCHODACK, ... "	"	"	
SCHENECTADY, ... "	"	1.50	
ST. JOHNSVILLE,.... "	"	"	
SANDY CREEK, ... "	"	"	
SAND BANKS,....... "	"	"	
SYRACUSE, ... "	.50	.88	
SHELDRAKE,........ "	"	"	
SKENEATELES,...... "	"	.87	
SENECA FALLS, ... "	"	"	
SHORTSVILLE, ... "	"	"	
STAFFORD, ... "	"	.63	
SAVANNAH,......... "	"	1.00	
SPENCERPORT, ... "	"	.75	
STARKEY, ... "	.75	1.00	
STITTSVILLE, ... "	.63	"	

Tariff of Rates from Buffalo or Suspension Bridge to	Bank Notes per $1000 — $600 Equal to $1000.	Freight per 100 lbs for 50 lbs and upwards.	Special Rates or Remarks.
SUFFERNS, ...N. Y.	.75	1.75	
SOUTHFIELD, ... "	"	"	
STOCKPORT, ... "	"	1.37	
SMITHBORO, ... "	"	1.00	
SWAINVILLE, ... "	"	.75	
SCIO, ... "	"	1.25	
SALAMANCA, ... "	"	1.37	
SMITH'S MILLS, ... "	"	1.50	
SAVONA, ... "	"	.87	
SPRING WATER, ... "	"	.75	
STATE LINE, ... "	1.50	2.00	
TROY, ...N. Y.	.75	2.00	
TARRYTOWN, ... "	"	"	
TIVOLI, ... "	"	"	
TRIBE'S HILL, ... "	.63	1.38	
TRENTON, ... "	"	"	
TABERG, ... "	.75	1.50	
THREE MILES BAY, . "	1.00	1.75	
TRUMANSBURGH, ... "	.50	1.00	

Tariff of Rates from Buffalo or Suspension Bridge, to	Bank Notes per $1000. / $600 Equal to $1000.	Freight per 100 lbs for 50 lbs and upwards.	Special rates or Remarks.
TONAWANDA, ... N. Y.	.25	.25	
TURNERS, ... "	.75	1.75	
TULLY, ... "	"	1.50	
UNION SPRINGS, ... N. Y.	.50	1.00	
UTICA, ... "	.63	1.25	
UNION, ... "	.75	"	
VERPLANCK, ... N. Y.	.75	2.00	
VERONA, ... "	.63	1.25	
VICTOR, ... "	.50	.75	
VIENNA, ... "	"	.87	
WEST POINT, ... N. Y.	.75	2.00	
WHITESBORO, ... "	.63	1.25	
WILLIAMSTOWN, ... "	.75	1.50	
WATERTOWN, ... "	"	"	

Tariff of Rates from Buffalo or Suspension Bridge to	Bank Notes per $1000. / $600 Equal to $1000.	Freight per 100 lbs for 50 lbs and upwards.	Special Rates or Remarks.
WAMPSVILLE, ...N. Y.	1.00	1.00	
WATKINS, ... "	.75	"	
WARNER'S SETTLM'T, "	.50	"	
WEST BLOOMFIELD, . "	"	.63	
WEEDSPORT, ... "	"	1.00	
WAVERLY, ... "	.75	"	
WELLSBURGH, ... "	"	"	
WASHINGTONVILLE, . "	"	1.75	
WATERLOO, ... "	.50	.87	
WARWICK, ... "	.75	1.75	
WHITNEY'S POINT, .. "	"	1.50	
WAYLAND, ... "	.87	.75	
WARSAW, ... "	.75	.50	
WENDE, ... "	"	"	
YONKERS, ...N. Y.	.75	2.00	
GOODWINVILLE, ...N. J.	.75	1.75	
HOHOKUS, ...N. J.	.75	1.75	

Tariff of Rates from Buffalo or Suspension Bridge to	Bank Notes per $1000. / $600 Equal to $1000.	Freight per 100 lbs for 50 lbs and upwards.	Special Rates or Remarks.
Patterson, ... N. J.	1.00	1.75	
Ramseys, ... N. J.	1.00	1.75	
Great Bend, ... Penn.	.75	1.25	
Lackawaxen, ... "	"	1.75	
Mast Hope, ... "	"	1.50	
Shohola, ... "	"	1.75	
Susquehanna, ... "	"	1.37	
Ashuelot, ... N. H.	1.75	2.50	
Hinsdale, ... N. H.	1.75	2.50	
Keene, ... N. H.	1.75	2.50	
Swansey, ... N. H.	1.75	2.50	

Tariff of rates from Buffalo or Suspension Bridge, to	Bank Notes per $1,000. $600 Equal to $1000.	Freight per 100 lbs. for 50 lbs. and upwards.	Special Rates or Remarks.
WINCHESTER, ...N. H.	1.75	2.50	
WESTPORT, ... "	"	"	
BECKET, ... Mass.	.50	2.75	
BOSTON, (*Local rate*,) "	1.75	2.50	
BERNARDSTON, ... "	"	"	
BERKSHIRE, ... "	1.50	2.25	
CHESTER FACTORIES, Mass.	1.50	2.25	
COLLIN'S DEPOT,.... "	1.75	2.50	
CHARLTON,......... "	"	"	
CLAPPVILLE, ... "	"	"	
CHICOPEE, ... "	"	"	
CHESIRE, ... "	1.50	2.25	
DALTON, ...Mass.	1.50	2.25	
DEERFIELD, ... "	1.75	2.50	
DUMMERSTON, ... "	"	"	
EAST BROOKFIELD,..Mass.	1.75	2.50	

Tariff of Rates from Buffalo or Suspension Bridge to	Bank Notes per $1000. — $600 Equal to $1000.	Freight per 100 lbs for 50 lbs and upwards.	Special Rates, or Remarks.
Framingham, ...Mass.	1.75	2.50	
Greenfield, ...Mass.	1.75	2.50	
Hinsdale, ...Mass.	1.75	.250	
Huntington, ... "	1.50	2.25	
Holyoke, ... "	1.75	2.50	
Hatfield, ... "	"	"	
Indian Orchard, ...Mass.	1.75	2.50	
Northampton, ...Mass.	1.75	.250	
North Adams, ... "	1.50	2.25	
Pittsfield, ...Mass.	1.50	2.25	
Palmer, ... "	1.75	2.50	
Packards, ... "	"	"	
Richmond, ...Mass.	1.50	2.00	
Russell, ... "	"	2.25	

Tariff of Rates from Buffalo or Suspension Bridge to	Bank Notes per $1000 / $600 Equal to $1000.	Freight per 100 lbs for 50 lbs and upwards.	Special Rates or Remarks.
SPRINGFIELD, (LOCAL RATE.). Mass.	1.75	2.50	
SPENCER, ... "	"	"	
SMITH'S FERRY,..... "	"	"	
SOUTH DEERFIELD,.. "	"	"	
SOUTH ADAMS,...... "	1.50	2.25	
SOUTH BROOKFIELD, "	1.75	2.50	
WEST PITTSFIELD,.. Mass.	1.50	2.00	
WASHINGTON, ... "	"	2.25	
WESTFIELD,........ "	"	"	
WEST SPRINGFIELD,. "	1.75	2.50	
WEST BROOKFIELD,. "	"	"	
WARREN, ... "	"	"	
WORCESTER, ... "	"	"	
WILLIAMSETT, ... "	"	"	
WHATELY, ... "	"	"	
WILLIAMSTOWN, ... "	1.50	2.25	
BRATTLEBORO,...... Vt.	1.75	2.50	
BELLOWS' FALLS,... "	"	"	

Tariff of Rates from Buffalo or Suspension Bridge to	Bank Notes per $1000. — $600 Equal to $1000.	Freight per 100 lbs for 50 lbs and upwards.	Special rates or Remarks.
EAST PUTNEY, ... Vt.	1.75	2.50	
PUTNEY, ... Vt.	1.75	2.50	
SOUTH VERNON, ... Vt.	1.75	2.50	
VERNON, ... Vt.	1.75	2.50	
WESTMINSTER, ... Vt.	1.75	2.50	
COBURG, ...C. W.	.50	1.00	
COLBORNE, ... "	"	"	
KINGSTON, ... "	1.00	1.75	
PORT HOPE, ... "	.50	1.00	
[illegible]	50	100	[illegible]
[illegible]	50	100	[illegible]

FROM Como Ill TO	Bank Notes per $1000 / $600 Equal to $1000.	Freight per 100 lbs for 50 lbs and upwards.	Special Rates or Remarks.
Granville Wis	100	200	
Bassetts	"	225	
Fox River	"	"	
Brooklyn	"	"	
Greenbush	125	200	
Brookfield	"	250	
Doylestown	"	300	
S. Addleton	"	275	

FROM Como Ill TO	Bank Notes per $1000. — $600 Equal to $1000.	Freight per 100 lbs for 50 lbs and upwards.	Special rates or Remarks.

FROM Cairo Ill TO	Bank Notes per $1000. $600 Equal to $1000.	Freight per 100 lbs for 50 lbs and upwards.	Special Rates or Remarks.

FROM Cairo Ill TO	Bank Notes per $1000. $600 Equal to $1000.	Freight per 100 lbs for 50 lbs and upwards.	Special Rates or Remarks.

FROM Como Ill TO	Bank Notes per $1,000. — $600 Equal to $1000.	Freight per 100 lbs. for 50 lbs. and upwards.	Special Rates or Remarks.

FROM Como Ill TO	Bank Notes per $1000. / $600 Equal to $1000.	Freight per 100 lbs for 50 lbs and upwards.	Special Rates, or Remarks.

FROM Como Ill TO	Bank Notes per $1000 / $600 Equal to $1000.	Freight per 100 lbs for 50 lbs and upwards.	Special Rates or Remarks.

FROM Como Ill TO	Bank Notes per $1000. / $600 Equal to $1000.	Freight per 100 lbs for 50 lbs and upwards.	Special rates or Remarks.

www.ingramcontent.com/pod-product-compliance
Lightning Source LLC
LaVergne TN
LVHW021408110826
845150LV00007B/1838

* 9 7 8 1 4 2 5 5 1 1 5 5 5 *